WORKING ABROAD ADDENDUM

Chapter 3 Taxation

The whole basis on which tax as it applies to expatriates is currently under review. In July 1988 the Inland Revenue produced a 'consultative document' which proposes some radical changes. Most of this will affect non British residents in the UK but some of the proposals will make a difference to British expatriates, particularly those overseas for a relatively short period and those overseas largely to avoid a short term capital gains tax liability. While it is conceivable that some of the proposals may be enacted in 1989, it is thought extremely unlikely that these will take immediate effect as a transitional period is almost certainly required. In the meantime we must continue to deal with the present legislation. It may be that when the next edition of Working Abroad is produced we will have a new system to get used to.

However, before this document was published the 1988 Budget had already made many changes in the UK tax scene. These are summarised below along with the new tax rates and personal allowances.

1. Basic rate of income tax is cut to 25% (following this the UK tax deduction from non exempt interest payments is reduced to 25% and the tax credit on UK corporate dividends is now 33⅓%).

2. A single higher rate of income tax of 40% on all taxable income over £19,300.

3. Personal reliefs for British expatriates (see pp31 et seq) will be available in full against UK income regardless of worldwide income from 1990/91 (when women will also be taxed as individuals for both earned and investment income plus capital gains).

4. Deeds of Covenant (see pp32 et seq) are no longer tax effective except in favour of charity.

5. The capital gains tax exemption is reduced to £5,000 for 1988/89 and taxable gains over this threshold are taxed at the individual's marginal income tax rate, i.e. 25%, 40% or part at 25% and the balance at 40%. From 1990/91 husband and wife will be taxed separately for capital gains tax purposes. The other major CGT change introduced is to take out of account gains made prior to 31st March 1982. What this means is, that for gains made after 5th April 1988, the gain is the difference between selling and buying price (allowing for indexation, etc.) or the selling price and the value at 31st March 1982 for assets held at that time.

6. The multiple rate structure of inheritance tax has also been changed and replaced with a single rate of 40% which applies to taxable transfers in excess of £110,000.

Key rates and allowances — 1988/89

Income tax

Taxable income	Slice	Rate	Total tax
£	£	%	£
19,300	19,300	25	4,285
Over 19,300		40	

Income tax allowances

Personal allowance — married	£4,095
single	£2,605
Wife's earnings allowed — maximum	£2,605
Life assurance relief — only on pre-14 March	
1984 policies	15%
Additional personal relief for children	£1,490
Age allowance — single	£3,180
married	£5,035
Age 80 or over — single	£3,310
married	£5,205
income limit	£10,600
Widow's bereavement allowance	£1,490

Capital gains tax

Rate (individuals)	25%/40%
Annual exemption (individuals etc.)	£5,000

Inheritence tax

Band £	Death rate %
0 — 110,000	Nil
110,001 upwards	40
Annual exemption	£3,000

VAT

Rate	15%
Registration threshold from 16.3.88	£22,100

Chapter 5 Investment and financial planning

Pension planning
For expatriates who do not belong to their company (either UK or overseas) pension plan there is now available an easily administered corporate scheme from Eagle Star which is treated both in the UK and in several other countries as a proper pension fund and which can be continued following the expatriate's return to the UK. This plan requires the employer's participation and, where the employer does not wish to contribute directly to the scheme, this may be overcome by a salary sacrifice on the part of the expatriate in order to build up his tax free investment.

Offshore Funds
Given the reduction in the capital gains tax allowance and the equation of capital gains tax and income tax rates, funds without distributor status maybe seen as more relevant now than they were prior to the 1988 Budget. For an investor who is likely to make use of his capital gains exemption elsewhere there is now no disadvantage in using non distributor funds. Given that this then increases the scope of selection for investors, it may be one of the better results of the capital gains tax changes.

Chapter 6 UK property
Another budget bombshell this year was the removal from tax relief of loans used for the improvement as opposed to the purchase of property. Secondly, the position whereby two unmarried individuals could purchase a property and each receive tax relief of up to £30,000 where the mortgage was £60,000 or more has also been changed. Now only £30,000 can be relieved regardless of how many mortgagors are involved in the one property. This does not, however, alter the relief available against rented property which can, in any event, exceed £30,000.

Chapter 10 Further information
Chapter 5 — Investment and financial plannng

The International
The Financial Times Business Information
Greystoke Place
Fetter Lane
London EC4A 1ND

October 1988

WORKING ABROAD —
THE EXPATRIATE'S GUIDE

How to live, work and invest abroad – a complete monthly guide

If you can resist anything but temptation then you may be planning to succumb to the lure of living abroad.

After all, what prospect could be more inviting than a warmer climate, a better job, a higher standard of living, more money and lower taxes.

Once you've made your move, or while you are seriously considering the possibility, you should know that there is only one truly authoritative guide for expatriates.

It is called Resident Abroad and from Bournemouth to Botswana its contents are eagerly devoured by thousands who have decided to enjoy the life of an expatriate.

The secret of a successful move

Above all else Resident Abroad is a 'how to' guide packed with detailed financial advice and information.

From the complications of efficient tax planning to the niceties of local custom, no other publication will be of such practical assistance.

When you want to know the best way to arrange diplomatic protection, the most effective method of moving your goods and chattels half way around the world, or the correct business protocol to adopt in Japan, you'll find yourself turning to Resident Abroad.

More than this you'll be kept informed about what is happening back home. Not the news as reported in the media but the things which are really important to you when you're abroad. You'll be surprised how interested you become in the cost of living (monthly shopping basket section) or in the property market when you've been away for a few months.

All in all Residents Abroad is a vital ingredient to the successful move.

Money matters

Since one of the primary benefits of waving goodbye – even temporarily – to the off-white cliffs of Dover, is that you're more likely to be far, far wealthier, the importance of sound financial advice cannot be stressed enough.

Resident Abroad not only carries numerous articles by leading offshore tax and investment experts, but will also help you find professional advisors to handle your personal affairs.

Free trial issue

Why not judge its contents for yourself? Send for a free issue without obligation to:
Financial Times Magazines,
Resident Abroad,
Greystoke Place,
Fetter Lane,
London EC4A 1ND,
UK.

WORKING ABROAD — THE EXPATRIATE'S GUIDE
3rd Edition

DAVID YOUNG

Financial Times Business Information

First published April 1983
Second edition November 1984
Third edition October 1987

Edited by Anthony Capstick

Published by FT Business Information Ltd
7th Floor, 50-64 Broadway, London SW1H 0DB
Registered number 980896

ISBN 1 85334 005 7

Typeset by New Rush Filmsetters Limited, London
Printed by The Camelot Press plc, Shirley Road, Southampton

About the author
David Young is a graduate of the University of St Andrew's and his early career was spent with the Inland Revenue. In 1976 he was appointed Deputy Editor in Chief of the Tolley Publishing Co Ltd where he wrote widely on UK tax and was the author of the 1977 edition of *Tolley's Taxation in the Channel Islands and the Isle of Man*.

In 1979 he became Deputy Editor of *Money Management* magazine and the founding editor of *Resident Abroad*, the Financial Times magazine for British expatriates. He has also written and contributed to several other Financial Times publications including *The Expatriate Survival Kit, The Expatriate's Guide to Savings & Investment, The Offshore Fund Yearbook*, and *Retiring Abroad*.

At the end of 1982 David Young left *Resident Abroad* to establish an independent advisory service for expatriates and their employers. He is now Managing Director of International Tax & Investment Planning in Cambridge. He continues to write for several expatriate publications and is a regular speaker at expatriate conferences.

Contents

Preface

In the Preface to the first edition of this book (reprinted overleaf) I described the British expatriate as an ordinary man or woman doing an ordinary job in an out-of-the-ordinary place. That remains true. It is also true that the bulk of the problems faced by expatriates are ordinary problems; but in the four and a half years since the first edition was written there have been some major changes in the expatriate world. The continuing low level of oil prices has led to a major reduction in the numbers of British expatriates employed in the Middle East; the Conservative government, re-elected yet again, continues to chop away at UK tax rates thereby reducing, if not eliminating, one of the oft quoted reasons for leaving the UK.

On the investment front the last four years have seen a mixture of good and bad — good in that markets generally have produced substantial profits for investors, and bad in that there has been a new crop of fraudulent practices including the sale of non existent stocks by high pressure telephone salesmen. In the UK, investor protection is very much the flavour of the month and the Financial Services Act will come fully into force in 1988. It would be an exaggeration to suggest that the passing of this act has resulted in a mass exodus of expatriate advisors from the UK to the perhaps less rigorously regulated regions of the world including Cyprus and Gibraltar. However, the act should mean that expatriates dealing with UK based advisors are more adequately protected than has been the case in the past.

Over the last four years I have travelled many hundreds of thousands of miles to speak to and advise British expatriates on their financial planning. During that time several new expatriate publications have been launched and, as a result, today's expatriates can be better informed than ever before. However, no magazine can provide answers to the almost infinite variety of questions and dilemmas posed by such a diverse group as Britons abroad. Neither can this book. But what it can do, hopefully, is give the expatriate sufficient information to be able to proceed in the right direction and ask the right questions of the right advisor.

This third edition of Working Abroad — The Expatriate's Guide is again dedicated to British expatriates everywhere. Not only do they provide me with my livelihood but also with readily given friendship and hospitality.

11 Millers Yard DAVID YOUNG
Mill Lane *20th July 1987*
Cambridge

Give us 2 weeks to sharpen your business edge.

"If you're serious about international business, the Financial Times is written specifically for you."

This statement, from a senior Morgan Guaranty executive, tells you better than we ever could why so many top European decision makers rely upon us for insight, analysis and hard business news.

Indeed, 38.5% of Europe's Chief Executives read the F.T. daily. In comparison, only 23.7% read our closest rival.*

No wonder we're first choice. With nearly 300 editorial staff worldwide and our own team of economists, analysts and statisticians – no one gives the complete picture of international business the way we do.

We keep you in touch with every political, commercial or financial development that can affect Europe's markets – and your business.

You'll find our International Edition is written specifically for European business leaders like you. With three full-time correspondents in France,

five in Germany and one in almost every Western European city, we can give you better insight, more impartial coverage.

And we can give them to you when it counts – we go to press in Frankfurt at 23.00 hrs., long after most European papers are printed. You get late-breaking stories. While you still have time to act.

If you read the F.T. daily, you get the insight you need to stay in tune with your market – and ahead of your competitors.

*The findings of a survey of European chief executives, jointly sponsored by the *Wall Street Journal* and *Business Week* – published April 1986.

12 ISSUES FREE

Take out you first subscription to the Financial Times and we'll send you 12 issues free. Then see for yourself why William Ungeheuer, *Time* magazine's senior financial correspondent, described us as "the paper with the best coverage of international finance".

To subscribe to the Financial Times or for more information send your name, address and telephone no. to: The Subscriptions Department, Financial Times (Europe) Ltd., Guiollettstrasse 54, D-6000 Frankfurt am Main 1, West Germany or telephone: Frankfurt (069) 75980.

Preface to the First Edition

The working British expatriate is not an exotic or extraordinary species. Neither is he possessed of extraordinary wealth, nor does he live the life of 'Riley' by some sun-kissed lagoon. Rather, he is an ordinary man (or woman) doing an ordinary job in an out-of-the-ordinary place. But what most expatriates have in common is a certain independence of spirit, the capacity for hard work, and a dread of the Inland Revenue.

Most people become expatriates in order to improve the quality of their lives, either immediately or in the future, through new and wider experience or by earning and saving more than is generally possible in the UK. A new lifestyle brings new problems but, in the main, they are still ordinary problems. This book has been written to help solve the ordinary problems of expatriate life.

Working Abroad — the Expatriate's Guide is a book written for the ordinary man. It is not aimed at the financial specialist (although he might learn something from it), nor is it aimed solely at the very high earning senior managers (although they might save money by using it), nor, finally, is it aimed at the pensioner thinking of retiring to the Costa del Sol. It is written for the average working expatriate who is either currently abroad or still contemplating the move. It attempts to cover all the main problem areas, including the technical and complex subject of UK tax, in as simple but comprehensive a way as possible. It will not answer every question that an expatriate can ask, but it should at least point him in the right direction.

Over the last four years, as Editor of *Resident Abroad*, I have greatly enjoyed meeting and corresponding with British expatriates in many countries. This book is for them and their successors and I look forward to meeting many more of them in the years ahead.

Great Chesterford
Essex

DAVID YOUNG
31st December 1982

1

Introduction

While unemployment in the UK is now falling it remains a major problem for more than two and half million Britons. It is hardly surprising therefore that employment abroad remains an attractive proposition. But in common with any job opportunities which arise in the UK, advertised vacancies abroad produce an enormous number of applicants. No longer are a basic qualification, a British passport, and a desire to travel sufficient to ensure a ticket on the next boat or plane to the chosen destination. Today, high unemployment is widespread and it is not only the British who wish to work away from home — competition for expatriate jobs will come from all quarters. The expatriate employer can afford to pick and choose his staff from a much bigger selection than ever before. Nonetheless, and fortunately for our home-grown potential expatriate, British skills and training remain much in demand and the fact that we often cost less to attract abroad, certainly compared to Americans and most other Europeans, is a further helpful factor.

Making the decision to look for work overseas may, in itself, be simple enough but, before giving any practical effect to the decision, it is essential to think carefully about all the aspects of such a move and about the particular consequences for the family. Much of this book is concerned with family matters and with the problems and opportunities that expatriate life will bring. Experience has shown that most expatriate failures, such as early return or inability to do the job properly, are caused by difficulties in family life. Thus it is important that all members of the family are fully aware of what lies in store for them and are agreed on the desirability of the move. Some of the most experienced employers of expatriates have long realised the importance of involving the whole family in discussions and briefings about an overseas posting. In many cases such companies are rewarded with a much lower expatriate turnover and, in consequence, a great saving in costs. Expatriate failure for whatever reason is invariably expensive, both in direct cash terms and in terms of efficiency in the overseas operation. The price of adequate early preparation is small and can prove to be an invaluable investment for both employer and employee. *Working Abroad — the Expatriate's Guide,* along with the other publications and the organisations mentioned in subsequent chapters, can all help in this preparation.

Getting a job, settling in to a new environment, and keeping the family happy are obviously essential parts of an expatriate success story. But there is another aspect to a job abroad which is of equal importance. One of an expatriate's main reasons for going abroad in the first place is probably to make money and acquire capital. Apart from the obvious consideration of salary, the new expatriate should have already made sure of several financial arrangements some time before leaving home. I make no apology for devoting the bulk of this book to financial matters because it is in this area that most advice is required and where the unwary may come badly unstuck. Obviously in any book it would be impossible to cover every eventuality but in chapters 3 to 6 and in chapter 8 all the main financial angles are covered as well as some of those that are more esoteric. Most expatriates realise fairly quickly that they need good professional advice, but even then they may have missed some opportunities.

Advice is needed before leaving the UK, during the overseas period, before returning home, and, where substantial sums of money have been saved, after returning to the UK.

There is no shortage of expatriate advisors based either in Britain or abroad. Some are very good, most are adequate, and one or two should be avoided. Guidelines for chosing an advisor are given in the chapter on financial planning. When faced with one of the many itinerant advisors, the expatriate's watchwords should be caution and a degree of cynicism — unfair as this might be to the many honest brokers it is necessary because of the rising numbers of 'advisors' who are simply not up to the job.

Finally, to return to the question of preparation before going overseas, chapter 9 provides some outline guidance for the new or intending expatriate on particular aspects of life in various parts of the world. However, it must be stressed that this is purely an outline and is no substitute for a proper background briefing and personal research. Organisations which can assist with full briefings are listed in the sources of further information in chapter 10.

Working Abroad does not provide all the answers to every question a British expatriate will ask, but it will have succeeded in its aim if it answers most and prompts the reader to question himself and enjoy his overseas life to the full in the knowledge that he is well-advised and well-prepared.

A great Manx bank and no tales.

We cannot tell a lie. Tyndall Bank is one of the top specialist banks for overseas depositors. To find out why we're the cat's whiskers, contact Barry Tippett on (0624) 29201. Tyndall Bank (Isle of Man) Limited, Tyndall House, Kensington Road, Douglas, Isle of Man.

Tyndall
A RATHER SPECIAL SERVICE

2

Getting a job abroad

THE EXPATRIATE JOB MARKET

One hundred years ago, when the world map showed a pre-ponderance of red, and not the red of communism, any young Briton with a degree of initiative could venture forth to make his fortune in the Empire. Today, the Empire is no longer with us and the young Briton no more enjoys a worldwide fiefdom than does the Frenchman, the German, or, indeed, anyone else. But Britain is still a great people exporter and demand for British skills and manpower is strong in both the developed and the developing world. A recent Foreign Office estimate put the number of new expatriates (not permanent emigrants) at about 200,000 each year but with the reduction in job opportunities at home this figure may well be on the low side.

Location

Where, then, do these 200,000 go and what do they do? Since the early seventies the Middle East, particularly Saudi Arabia, and Western Europe have attracted most British expatriates, but a British presence can be found in virtually every country in the world. *Resident Abroad* — The Financial Times magazine for British expatriates — has readers in 168 countries. However, as mentioned in the preface to this edition, the Middle East over the last year or two has shown a net reduction in British expatriate employees. That is not to say that there are no longer opportunities in that part of the world, but with the belt tightening exercises of the major Gulf states the expatriate profile has changed. Many jobs previously the almost exclusive preserve of Britons are now carried out by Asians, particularly in middle manage-ment areas in the commercial sector. In general, contracts for all but the most senior and highly qualified people are shorter, there is a reduction in the number of married status posts and salaries are in most cases significantly lower than they were a few years ago — both in local terms and in sterling. Apart from the areas already mentioned, there are many expatriate opportunities in Africa — mainly Nigeria, Zambia, Kenya and South Africa, and to a lesser extent in the North African countries of Algeria and Libya. In the Far East, Hong Kong, Singapore, Malaysia and Indonesia are the main expatriate centres but Britons are far from being thin on the ground in Papua New Guinea, Brunei and many other Pacific Islands. In the western hemisphere the United States is very popular with the British but is also one of the most difficult countries in which to obtain work. Entry to Canada is easier and this country is still seen as offering one of the best prospects

3

for the British expatriate. The various British enclaves in the Caribbean, both Commonwealth members and remaining colonies, do not attract significant numbers of short-term expatriates but remain popular with the long-term expatriates and the permanent emigrants.

Type of employment

Turning to the question of expatriate employment and what the British expatriate does, the simple answer is, everything. Expatriate jobs encompass everything from butler to banker, engineer to engine driver, nurse to national guardsman, and computer operator to comptroller of a treasury. However, the expatriate market is changing and the requirements of each country do, of course, vary. Expatriate jobs in the unskilled or semi-skilled categories are now a thing of the past except, occasionally, in some European countries. Skilled tradesmen, particularly in building work, are still in demand in the Middle East and some African countries but this demand is declining. Most expatriate jobs now are for professionally qualified people — engineers, technologists, medical, finance and administrative staff, and teachers.

In the oil states there is a continuing, albeit reduced, demand for expatriate labour in the oil industry at the technological and managerial level. As a result of the past oil wealth, there is still a demand for development in the infrastructure of the countries — construction of all sorts, communications and administration. Alongside this, and possibly offering the best chance of continuing expatriate involvement, is the development of new industries and services against the time when the oil runs out. New developments include high technology, banking and financial services, general trading and process industries. Apart from the individual specialists required for each of these, the expatriate entrepreneur may now find himself much more welcome than in the past.

In many of the major non-oil-producing expatriate centres the emphasis is still on primary production, either in the agricultural field or in mining. This is true of much of Africa and the Far East. Throughout the developing world there are also jobs for expatriate medical staff at all levels — doctors, nurses, technicians, and teachers for schools and universities. Administrative posts in both government and private sectors are also widely available to the British expatriate. In Europe, expatriate opportunities are available across the whole spectrum of business but a major source of jobs is to be found in the international civil service. Posts are legion in the EEC Commission but other organisations such as NATO, the UN and its offshoots, the Red Cross and others also recruit from Britain. In the USA, expatriate jobs are severely limited at the present time and where they are available they are almost exclusively related to the electronics and aerospace industries at a high professional level. Recently the American medical profession has been recruiting quite heavily in the UK and the Republic of Ireland particularly for nurses and junior medical staff.

To sum up, the market in expatriate jobs is still very healthy although competition for the jobs themselves makes it harder for the individual to obtain the job and location of his choice. One final

Raising the standard of international investment.

If you're planning to live, work or retire abroad you'll want your savings and investments to take full advantage of your special tax position.

We specialise in providing assurance, investment and personal trust services for expatriates and residents abroad.

Ætna is one of the world's largest insurance and investment groups. Our global investment management network is responsible for over $120 billion of funds for our corporate and private clients.

To find out how Ætna International can raise the standard of your investments, please return the coupon today.

Or telephone our Customer Services Centre at our Guernsey office on 0481 27066 or Paula Barron in London on 01 837 6494.

point which is, I believe, often overemphasised — how long will this market last? The question is most commonly raised in the context of the developing countries, where the expatriate employer is often told that the number of work permits available to him will be steadily (or, on occasion, precipitately) reduced. Obviously, to stay in business the employer must train local staff to take over from the expatriates — the object of the exercise from the host country's point of view. This undoubtedly worthy aim can, however, have other consequences, particularly in a developing economy. An example from the Middle East illustrates a not uncommon situation. In 1980 an expatriate general manager was told that within two years his entitlement to one hundred work permits for expatriate staff would be reduced to permits for two — himself and the finance director. All other staff were to be replaced by locals. Four years later he still had 100 expatriate employees. This is not an example of failure, it is quite the reverse. He had trained over 300 local employees to a professional level of competence who, as soon as they were trained, left to work with other companies in the same country. His 'nursery' had provided most of the local technicians for two new ventures and some of his original expatriates had also moved over; but he still employed as many expatriates as before. By mid-1987, following largely on the general recession in the Middle East, this manager now employs only 50 expatriates. This, however, is due to reduced working and a general slow down in orders from within the region, and there is no question that when the local economy picks up, as is assumed over the next, say, five years, he will return to his 100 expatriates.

Finding the right job

As the first part of this chapter has indicated, expatriate jobs are readily available. But the desire to live in Bahrain or Bangkok and the intention of making lots of money, although perhaps necessary conditions, are certainly not sufficient conditions to ensure finding the right job. After obtaining a general picture of expatriate opportunities, the first thing the would-be expatriate should do is indulge in some rigorous self-analysis.

This advice may be appropriate to anyone changing jobs, whether within the UK or elsewhere, but it is of much greater relevance and much more important when the change involves not only new employment but a new lifestyle and a whole new culture. It happens not infrequently that someone sees a job which seems suitable and at that point asks himself if it is what he wants. At that point it is usually too late. What can commonly happen is that a process of selective censorship and rationalisation comes into play and the facts are fitted round the job rather than the job being selected to fit the facts. Self-assessment has to come first.

To be useful, self-assessment must be done honestly. Its aim is to give the potential expatriate a realistic and realisable goal in terms both of the type of job he will be able to do and of his aptitude for the different life he can expect to lead overseas. In assessing himself, the individual will certainly list his experience and achievements in education, training, present and previous employments. Problem areas or particular shortcomings in any of these should also be noted. From this should come a good indication of particular strengths.

A more difficult part of the assessment comes with an analysis of character and personality. As Burns wrote, 'O wad some Pow'r the giftie gie us, to see oursels as others see us, it wad frae mony a blunder free us, and foolish notion'. Few of us are able to be fully objective about ourselves but we should be able to say whether we are sociable or solitary, easy going or emotional, thick or thin skinned and an individualist or a follower. It might be thought that a successful expatriate should be a sociable, easy-going, self-confident individualist but it does not always follow. The adage 'horses for courses' applies as much to expatriates as to anyone else. What is important is to know the main personal traits.

As part of the self-assessment procedure much attention must be paid to family involvement. Spouses, children and other dependants must be considered, as must their own individual commitments and their aptitude for life abroad, or alternatively, for life at home while the breadwinner is abroad.

Where the self-analysis presents an acceptable profile of ability and aptitude and there is no diagnosis of latent xenophobia, the next step is to set out fairly detailed aims and objectives. The first of these relates directly to the sort of job required. The ideal may be a particular job or type of job but it is useful to have a second string of jobs which are, if not ideal, at least acceptable. Beyond this second string the potential expatriate should be ruthless in his refusal to consider anything else. The attitude of 'Well, I'll take this and it might get better after a while' is a sure recipe for disaster.

So long as the original objective is realistic it is better to wait than to take on something unsuitable.

Similar comments apply to job location. Employment in France might be the ideal with Belgium, Germany or Italy an acceptable second best. It would be foolish in those circumstances to accept a post in Saudi Arabia or Indonesia just because it became available first.

As with job type and location, basic priorities and conditions should be laid down for the level of remuneration and other benefits.

The identification of realistic aspirations and objectives can be a lengthy process but it is in fact a major time saver in the long run. There are tens of thousands of overseas jobs advertised in Britain each year and the person with a clearly defined aim will be able to devote all his energies to following up only the ones of direct interest. In addition, at the interview stage he or she will be able to give a much more precise account of himself or herself than if all and sundry jobs were being considered.

Unfortunately, in a world where competition for almost every job is fierce and many applicants are simply desperate for a job, any job, methodical preparation and job selection often go by the board. That said, it can only be re-emphasised that as much preparation as possible can lead to better prospects with less time wasted in the end.

How to find overseas employment
When the background work, however briefly, has been done, the next

step is to locate the jobs themselves. The first port of call, often neglected, is the present employer. Many British businesses have overseas parent, associate, or subsidiary companies or other connections with overseas employers. An enquiry down this route may provide overseas work with the possible advantage of retaining or improving one's position with the original employer. Similarly, many British civil servants may be favourably considered for overseas posts with certain government agencies or for secondment to international or foreign government posts.

Going beyond the current employer, details of overseas jobs are to be found from many sources. Foremost of these are the national newspapers, both daily and weekly. The so-called quality press provides the bulk of these but the popular tabloids also have a share. Professional magazines and trade journals are another obvious source of supply for the specialist but there is often a great deal of duplication in these journals and the national press especially for the more senior positions. Many of the less senior jobs will also be advertised locally overseas and it may be worthwhile obtaining the principal magazines and weekly papers from the country concerned. The one disadvantage in applying to this source, however, is that locally advertised jobs will often be subject to local interviews which may involve the applicant in some considerable expense. Another source of overseas job advertisements is *Executive Post* published by PER (Professional & Executive Recruitment) Overseas (see chapter 10).

Apart from published advertisements, the would-be expatriate employee may find his niche through recruitment agencies, search consultants (headhunters), professional associations and, from time to time, by a direct approach to a particular employer.

The mechanics of applying for an expatriate job are much the same as those for any domestic job. What may be slightly different is the emphasis to be given to certain aspects of training or experience. Knowledge of languages, previous overseas service in whatever capacity, experience in training other people and apparent initiative and flexibility are likely to be of greater importance to an expatriate employer or agent than they might be for a UK based position. If selected for an interview, it is essential that the candidate does some homework on both the employer, if his identity is known, and the country in which he proposes working. Most recruitment agencies will tell stories of candidates who turn up for interviews without the least notion of where their proposed location is, let alone knowing anything else about it. They fail.

Most of this section could be described as basic good sense. I hesitate to use the expression 'common sense' because more often than not, what is so described may be sense and it may be logical, but is not all that common. Finding the right expatriate job is not easy but it can be made a great deal easier by adopting a methodical approach with self confidence engendered through proper preparation.

THE EXPATRIATE EMPLOYER
As expatriates come in all shapes and sizes, so too do their employers.

Take a look at Albany International's personalised investment accounts... ...then take a look at the funds on which they're based.

Four Major Offshore Accounts

Our new offshore investments are not called plans, bonds or policies. They are *accounts*, designed to operate like accounts in investment banking.

So what's in a name?

Well, Albany International accounts are managed on a more personal basis, giving investors and advisers greater freedom of control and better access to both services and information.

But the real revolution is in our new (and unique) charging structure. No percentage of fund charges. No escalating costs as you invest more. Instead, a fixed fee-based system that uses *100%* of your capital *from the outset*.

There are four accounts to choose from, with minimum investments from £2,500 (or £300 per month) to £25,000.

They offer many advantages, depending on your own priorities: flexible funding, capital conversion, tax-free benefits, a variety of income or profit-taking options – even planned investment schemes to fill the "pension gap" and provide a secure future.

We believe nobody does more to offer freedom, flexibility and growth potential to expatriate investors.

Look at the funds on which we base our accounts and you'll see why.

Fifteen Major International Funds

Managed by Mercury Asset Management Limited, our offshore funds combine the solid performance of established markets with the dynamism of successful new markets.

Global sterling and dollar funds provide a worldwide spread of high-potential equities. UK, European, North American and Japanese funds give investors the benefit of a select range of international stocks and shares. A bond/cash Fixed-Interest fund maximises returns from currency fluctuation, interest and bond-price movements. The UK Blue Chip Sterling Fund presents new opportunities for investment in the high-profile UK equity market. And two recent additions, the Pacific Basin Sterling/Dollar Funds offer access to the dynamic financial and industrial markets of Hong Kong, Singapore, Korea, Taiwan and Australia.

FLEXIBLE ACCOUNTS · FREEDOM OF CHOICE · OPTIMISED CAPITAL · A STRATEGIC SPREAD OF FUNDS

All from a member of one of the world's very largest financial organizations (the $100bn Metropolitan Life Group), based in one of the world's best regulated offshore centres – the Isle of Man.

Ask your financial adviser for Albany International's information pack.

Albany International

ALBANY INTERNATIONAL ASSURANCE LIMITED
St. Mary's, The Parade, Castletown, Isle of Man, British Isles.
Telephone: 0624 823262. Telefax: 0624 822560. Telex: 629889 ALINTL-G

ALBANY INTERNATIONAL ASSURANCE LIMITED
A SUBSIDIARY COMPANY OF MET LIFE U.K. – PART OF THE METROPOLITAN LIFE GROUP OF COMPANIES.
FUNDS MANAGED WITH ADVICE FROM MERCURY ASSET MANAGEMENT LTD.

NEW FREEDOM FOR THE EXPATRIATE INVESTOR.

However, within this multiplicity there are four main categories of employer: government, British-based companies, non-British-parented multinational companies, and local companies. Apart from working for an employer there can be opportunities for self-employment but in many countries this will still require a local partner or co-director and may thus be akin to working in the fourth category mentioned above.

Government employment

Under this heading can be grouped UK government employment with any department or agency from the Diplomatic Service and the armed forces to the British Council and the Overseas Development Administration (ODA). It will include also temporary secondment from, for example, the Inland Revenue to a tax administration in a developing country. Through its multifarious offices and agencies the British government is a major expatriate employer. Foreign governments, too, engage large numbers of British expatriates for both administrative and technical services and, often through the British Council, for academic posts at all levels.

A third type of government employment is with the international Government agencies. These range from regional bodies such as the EEC to worldwide organisations such as the UN and its associated groups, the IMF and the World Bank, the Red Cross, Amnesty International and so forth. This species of international civil servant has proliferated in recent years and looks set to continue to do so for some time to come. Employment within any of these government agencies, home, foreign, or international, is usually for a fixed term in any one country, although in home or international government service the overseas tour may be but a part of a continuing career development. Foreign government service is generally for a two year term renewable until such time as there is a properly qualified local replacement.

British-based companies

'Export or die' is an exhortation often made to British industry and the message has been well taken, not only recently but back in the days of Empire. In consequence there are many British expatriates around the world working directly for British employers or indirectly through local subsidiaries of British firms. Most are to be found in the extraction of raw materials — oil, minerals and other commodities, and in construction and communications. Many of the household names in British industry, BP, RTZ, Lonrho, Cable & Wireless and Wimpey for example, employ thousands of British and other expatriates. In addition to these heavy industries, businesses in the fields of electronics and computing, financial services, and catering and hotelkeeping are now also major expatriate employers. Since the lifting in 1979 of exchange control in the UK and the ending of the recession at home, more and more British companies have sought both markets and manufacturing bases abroad. Even that most British of institutions, Marks and Spencer, has expanded into Europe and North America.

Foreign-based multinationals

The tendency of multinational companies, British-based or otherwise, is to employ their own nationals in their home base but to recruit more widely for overseas operations. Generally there will be significant local recruitment backed by home country expatriates and 'third country nationals'. Companies employing the greatest number of third country nationals in skilled technical or managerial posts are the American-based multinationals. European, Japanese and other companies usually manage to fill most of these posts with their own expatriates but the American expatriate is a very expensive animal. European and particularly British staff can be much cheaper for American companies. In part this has been caused by the American's worldwide liability to American income tax; for him there has been no such thing as a totally tax-free salary. Recent changes in American Federal tax law have made some difference to this position but this has not had a major impact on expatriate employment prospects for Britons.

Local employers

Local employment is often to be found in the media, finance, specialist industries and general trading. In Europe and North America local employment can be across a wide field but, as already mentioned, obtaining employment in the USA is currently extremely difficult. Local employment in this context does not include working for many of the major industries in some countries since these are most often either government owned or are quasi-governmental.

The financial reward for local employment may be greater than that which is paid by the multinational — perhaps to compensate for the absence of the large company infrastructures and benefits such as pension schemes and the like. But on the other hand, if there is competition with the local labour market, the remuneration might be less than that offered by the big companies. Examples of the former abound in, for instance, Saudi Arabia and the latter is not uncommon in Hong Kong.

Employee status

One thing which almost all expatriate employers have in common is a consciousness of their employees' status in their country of operation — that of guest. This is particularly important where the employer is himself a guest. For that reason the most enlightened employers take care to brief their expatriates very carefully on what will be expected of them, not only on the job but socially as well. They will take care not to send an inveterate drinker and womaniser to Riyadh or a prudish innocent to Bangkok or Manila. More information on pre-departure briefing is given in chapter 9.

CONTRACT TERMS AND CONDITIONS

At first sight, contract terms and conditions for expatriates often appear extremely generous when compared to what is on offer for most UK jobs. Not only are salaries generally much higher but the range of fringe benefits can be extensive. On the other side of the coin are the often greater responsibility in a similarly designated job abroad, much longer hours than the UK norm, an alien and possibly difficult work and social environment and a certain amount of family upheaval. Expatriate employers are rarely given to undue generosity; every item in the package is there for a good reason.

Legal protection

Before discussing the terms which a potential expatriate should expect, it may be advisable to consider the actual contract itself. Employees in Britain are protected by a substantial volume of employment legislation, special courts and other machinery. The expatriate employee, even if he works for a British employer, is rarely covered by this legislation. It is necessary, therefore, for the expatriate to know under what legal system his contract is written and what legal redress he may have in the event of any non-performance or dispute. This fairly basic requirement can be remarkably clouded and will depend largely on the status of the employer. Each of the four main categories described in the previous section may give rise to different legal structures.

Where the appropriate legal system has been agreed, the potential employee should then examine his contract with the following considerations in mind. Foreign language contracts must be translated by a person familiar with the legal terms and jargon of that language — even the most fluent conversationalist is unlikely to be familiar with these. Check that there is a specific disputes procedure. The contract should specify the initial term of the employment and any terms and conditions relating to its renewal. Finally, and most obviously, the contract should provide all appropriate details of the job — its nature, title, hours to be worked, provision for overtime, leave, salary and all benefits in kind, and the extent of both responsibility and independence involved. This last point can be particularly necessary where the expatriate is the senior representative of his company in the country; he may be held liable for all the company's actions.

Hours of work

Turning now to the actual terms of the contract, it has already been noted that most expatriate jobs require longer hours and offer greater responsibility than their UK equivalents. A precise specification may not always be possible and the terms may be vague, along the lines of 'hours sufficient to ensure the proper performance of the duties'. While not wholly satisfactory, this sort of phraseology is not uncommon, even in the UK. In general terms the expatriate will find he works a longer day than the UK average of eight hours, and the two-day weekend may be nothing but a fond memory after a year abroad where 5½ or 6 days constitute the normal working week. Most expatriates in the developing world have a training responsibility either as part of a company-wide scheme or an individual programme to train a local replacement. Social responsibilities may also arise either explicitly or by implication. All in all, the expatriate will find

12

that his employment takes up much more of his time and energy than was the case in the UK.

Salary

But there are compensations for long hours and extra responsibilities. The structure of an expatriate pay and benefit package will vary according to the particular job, the employer, and to a certain extent, the employee, so only some broad guidelines can be given here. The salary component is commonly made up from several parts. The first of these will be either the local rate for the job or, in the case of employers themselves based outside the job location, the home rate for a similar job. This sum should then be adjusted to take account of any differences in living costs which the expatriate will experience *vis-à-vis* either the local workforce or his home-based equivalents. In addition, there may be an incentive payment to compensate for extra responsibility, longer hours, or possibly a hazardous or unpleasant environment. Finally there may be a terminal bonus or gratuity both to encourage the expatriate to serve out the term of his contract and/or to compensate him for the lack of any formal pension scheme.

Apart from the amount of salary actually paid it is important that the expatriate is aware of exactly how and where it is to be paid. Payment is normally made in one of three ways or in a combination of these ways. They are: payment to a UK bank, payment locally, or payment into a bank in a third country — commonly a tax haven or low tax area. Several factors will influence the method of payment and the value of the alternatives. For the employee himself the most important thing to consider is whether or not his money is, and will remain, freely available. Many countries operate some form of exchange control and in some cases these controls are highly restrictive and allow only partial repatriation of earnings. Where there are no restrictions of this sort then any of the alternatives listed above may be acceptable. But exchange control is notorious for the speed with which it can be applied or changed so some caution may still be advisable. Where there are exchange control problems then local payment of the total salary is to be avoided. Most employers are aware of this and will make arrangements accordingly. This usually involves the local payment of sufficient of the salary to meet normal living expenses, with the balance paid either in the home country or in a tax haven.

Whether or not the individual expatriate will have any say in these arrangements depends on the nature of his employment. Except at the most senior consultant level, jobs with governments or their agencies offer little flexibility. Companies locally based abroad will generally pay locally and this is particularly true in countries with restrictive exchange controls. Multinational companies offer the greatest scope and the more responsible the position the greater the chances are for the expatriate to dictate the method of payment most suitable to his own circumstances.

Another important point on salaries is the currency in which they are paid or computed. Overseas governments and local employers will almost invariably quote salaries in local currency. Other employers are likely to quote in their home currency although actual payment may be made in the local currency. What gives the expatriate employee the greatest protection is to have a 'salary split' whereby part of the salary is quoted in sterling, and the balance, equivalent to everyday expenditure, is quoted in local currency. In this way the employee has at least partial protection against currency fluctuations. He will not lose local purchasing power in the event of a sterling devaluation, nor will he find his surplus income eroded in the event of a local currency devaluation.

Where a currency-split salary is not available many employers will nonetheless undertake to adjust salaries following any major change in exchange rates between the employee's home currency and that in which he is paid. Where any adjustment acts to protect the employee's purchasing power it is rightly seen as a valuable safeguard. But where the employee has benefited from a change in exchange rates there is inevitably much reluctance to accept a realignment. Company practice varies in these circumstances; some permit the employee to enjoy this windfall, but may perhaps take it into account when computing any future salary increase, while others insist on making the readjustment immediately.

Fringe benefits
Fringe benefits, perks, or benefits in kind, whatever the label, are popular with British employees, encouraged by employers, and tolerated, with some reluctance, by the government and the Revenue. Apart from pension schemes and life assurance cover, the most common perks are subsidised meals, cars and medical insurance. For the expatriate the picture is quite different. Short and medium term expatriates, that is, those whose contracts are for between one and six years, rarely have any pension schemes unless they are seconded from a UK employer, but the other benefits are extensive. Unlike the home situation where benefits can often be regarded simply as extras, the expatriate benefit range is an integral and essential part of the total package. If a job in Singapore did not come with accommodation then the salary required by the expatriate would be astronomical, and if the married status post in Saudi did not include a car and driver then the expatriate wife would be a prisoner in her home. The expatriate is often faced with many expenses which do not arise at home and the apparent generosity of the benefit package simply reflects these extra expenses. Without the benefits the employers would have much greater difficulty in recruiting staff or would have to increase cash payments substantially. A list of the more common benefits and some comments on them is given below.

Accommodation
This is the most ubiquitous and the most important of expatriate benefits. A *Resident Abroad* survey in 1981 found that accommodation was provided either free or highly subsidised to nearly 80 per cent of expatriates. Western Europe and North America are the major exceptions; there, most expatriates are expected to find and fund their own accommodation although the employer will often assist with removals

and temporary lodgings. The more enlightened employers will either have on the staff, or will make use of, independent relocation specialists. Such people will have a good knowledge of the area concerned and will be able to provide potential new employees with full details of local accommodation, costs, schools, etc. UK multinationals generally have such a person on the staff whereas in the US it is most common to use a local relocation agency. As a rule, American-based employers are somewhat more reluctant to provide accommodation than their British and other European counterparts, except in areas where adequate housing is a major problem. Where accommodation is not provided, it is essential that the expatriate checks the current price of rental property. What may have seemed a high salary can be put into a completely different perspective when the first 30 per cent disappears on housing costs. If accommodation is supplied, it can be important to find out just what it is. If it is unfurnished then at least the employee knows what he must bring or buy on the spot and the employer, in that case, will usually provide some assistance with removals or the purchase of certain essentials.

It is where the property is described as furnished that most of the problems arise. What I would consider to be an adequately furnished apartment might not coincide with the perceptions of many of the readers of this book, nor would it necessarily agree with the ideas of many expatriate employers. As detailed an inventory as possible should be requested at the earliest opportunity. Only then can the intending expatriate make proper provision for what has to be taken along. But even an inventory is not foolproof. It is not unknown in some expatriate compounds for a vacant company house to be raided by other expatriates who want to replace their perhaps broken down or inadequate company furnishings with what has been left behind or what has been provided new for the incoming tenant.

Cars

Company cars are widely available to expatriates, with North America once again the main exception. In the USA and Canada, where a company vehicle is necessary, it is rarely made available for private motoring. Elsewhere cars are generally available much as in the UK but a company driver, also usually available for private functions, is not uncommon. A second car with or without driver may be provided for an expatriate wife. In Saudi Arabia a second car with driver is essential since women are not allowed to drive. Where cars are not provided some expatriate employers will assist with the purchase and/or importation of a vehicle.

Education

Where the employee has children of primary school age this benefit will normally comprise fees at a local English language or international school. Where these facilities are not available locally, UK boarding school fees may be paid, but in most cases boarding school fees are restricted to older children. In recent years, British school fees have risen dramatically and many employers no longer pay the full cost. Many place a ceiling of £2,500 to £3,000 per annum per child on this benefit, or agree to pay, say, 75 per cent of the fees. For the most expensive schools this can still leave the parents to find over £2,000 per child each year.

Travel and holidays
For the employee himself there is usually provided one round trip air fare each year for home leave. In the case of short term (one or two years) contracts, leave is often to be taken at the end of the term so this will not apply. In married or accompanied status posts the travel facility will also be extended to dependants. Where children are at school in the UK, however, there can be problems. Employer practice varies, with some only providing for air fares for children during the summer holidays, others providing two trips each year (most common), and others allowing trips each holiday. Where trips are restricted, travel can be a large burden on the expatriate family budget unless the children can be looked after by friends or relatives during some holidays.

Insurances
Life assurance and medical insurance are two essential requirements for every expatriate, whether provided by the employer or not. Where medical insurance comes as part of the remuneration package the employee should ensure that it covers all family members and that there are no major exclusions such as pregnancy and childbirth. Where only the expatriate employee is covered he should also make sure that the cover extends beyond the workplace and out of working hours. It is not unknown for an expatriate to find himself unprotected if he has an accident on the way from work to his home or if he falls ill on his day off. Wherever possible the insurance package should also provide for repatriation in the event of serious illness affecting any family member.

Pensions
Pension provision is unlikely to take the same form as with a UK employment unless the overseas appointment is simply a secondment from a UK company. In that case normal pension contributions would continue based on a notional UK salary for up to three years. Thereafter new arrangements would be made. Where the UK company retains control over the expatriate's movements, this may not constitute a proper secondment and the expatriate may stay within the UK pension scheme indefinitely. Some overseas employers make no provision whatever for their expatriate employees, leaving the matter entirely to the individual. Where there is an employer scheme and the expatriate joins it he should check the accessibility of his contribution or final entitlement. Will he be able to obtain his contributions as a lump sum on leaving the employment or will he have to wait until he reaches retirement, and at what age? He should also check what local tax liability, if any, attaches to the lump sum or pension. Where there is an expatriate pension scheme or terminal gratuity scheme in force, these will commonly not be separate from the business. The employer's ability to pay may often depend on the continuing profit-

ability of his business and his cash flow at the time the employee leaves. In recent years with the economic problems of the oil states many expatriates have found that their terminal gratuity or repayment of pension contributions has been postponed for some time. In most cases payment will be made perhaps six or even twelve months late. But in certain cases the gratuity can be lost entirely. Again it is well worth the potential employee's time to check out what redress under what legal system he may have in the event of non-payment.

Holidays
Although not strictly a benefit in kind, holidays may be conveniently mentioned in this section. Holiday entitlement is often dependent on local practice. Where the norm is two or three weeks each year as in North America, it is likely to be the same for expatriates. Other countries are more generous with leave, particularly those places with extremes of climate. Four to six weeks is common and eight weeks is not unusual. As already noted, employees with one or two year contracts are often expected to take their leave at the end of the period. In weighing up the amount of holiday it should be remembered that for many expatriates, with longer hours and shorter weekends, the working week is up to 50 per cent longer than is normal in Britain, so what might seem generous simply serves to redress the balance.

Unaccompanied (single) and accompanied (married) status jobs
Many expatriate jobs are designated 'unaccompanied posts' which means that only single people, or married people whose families are prepared to stay at home while the employee works overseas, need apply. Other jobs are designated 'accompanied posts' and are generally offered to married men on the assumption that their families will go abroad too. There are advantages and disadvantages in both types of appointment but what should always be remembered is that there is usually a very good reason for the employer making whichever stipulation and it is rarely a question of cost. Most employers take the view that an expatriate will settle in more quickly and be more effective in a post if he is accompanied by his family. The extra cost is relatively insignificant but the restriction against families may arise through actual or potential hazards — climate, disease, political instability, or because of the nature of the job, possibly in a remote area with only the most basic or primitive facilities. In some countries there may also be problems with residence permits.

Where a job has no status designation in this context it usually means either unaccompanied or accompanied at the employee's cost or by negotiation with the employer. Accompanied status posts sometimes imply that a couple is required, perhaps because of social requirements and entertaining. The validity of this should be checked beforehand, especially by couples whose previous social life has been restricted to close friends and relatives. The expatriate social whirl can be hectic.

Finally, some expatriates on single status contracts consider taking their families in any case and without their employer's sanction. This is not a wise move, at least until they have themselves been in the job for several months. By then they might realise why the job was designated single status in the first place.

OVERSEAS REMOVALS AND SETTLING IN

Removals

The majority of expatriates are provided with accommodation which is usually furnished at least to a basic level. Thus there is not always the need to export all one's goods and chattels to the new country. However, even when one is only concerned with the removal of personal effects and a few small items it is important to get it right. Overseas removals are complex and expensive and can rarely be done satisfactorily on a DIY basis. Overseas removers are never cheap but it is well worth paying for the experience of a good company (and in any case, the majority of expatriate employers will be paying some part of the cost as a relocation expense). The overseas section of the British Association of Removers will advise on member companies with appropriate experience.

Whether the total house contents or only a part of them are to be taken abroad, packing can present a problem. As a general rule it is better to allow the remover to do it all. Not only should he have all the proper packing materials, but if he does the job the insurance cost in transit should be lower than if the intending expatriate does it himself. More important than who does the packing is what, in fact, has to be packed. For a move to furnished accommodation the requirements are likely to be only some soft furnishings and small electrical appliances (if they are compatible with the local supply). Where a full removal is necessary, it is important to check the price and availability of the larger items locally since the cost of purchase may not be much more than the removal cost. In any case the individual should be quite ruthless about what can be disposed of or left behind — junk at home is just as likely to be junk abroad.

There are two basic methods of getting your effects abroad — by air or by sea or sea/road/rail. The cost of air-freight is very high and the sea route is most common. In some cases where the expatriate and his family would have to stay in a hotel until the arrival of their furniture it may be cheaper to pay the extra cost of air-freight than the hotel bills. When a transit time is quoted for sea-freight make sure that it is not only the time actually spent at sea but an estimate of total time from packing to eventual customs clearance.

Storage

Where a full removal is not necessary there arises the question of storage of furniture and effects for the duration of the overseas tour. There is no problem if the UK home is to be let fully-furnished in the owner's absence or if the home is to be held available for home leaves, children's holidays and the like. In other cases furniture must either be sold or stored. Most removal firms will have either their own storage facilities or access to a central repository. Storage costs are about £1.00 to £1.25 per 100 cubic feet per week which means for the contents of an average three-bedroomed house the annual cost will be in the region of £500. In addition there will be the cost of the removal to store, insurance while goods are stored and eventual removal costs from store.

What to take and what to leave behind
There are many items which require particular care or an early decision on whether or not they should be taken abroad. These are described briefly below.

Electrical goods
The first thing to be checked is the voltage of the overseas electricity supply. If this differs from the UK supply (250V, 50Hz) the appliances may be unusable unless they have voltage adjusters. A further point to consider is the availability of servicing facilities abroad; if there are none, then the appliance should be left behind or disposed of. Many major appliances such as cookers, refrigerators and washing machines are standard fixtures in modern accommodation especially in North America and Europe. With the exception of South Africa, television sets should not be taken abroad since they will require extensive modification before being usable.

Gas appliances
These should rarely be taken abroad. Supply pressure, type of gas and service facilities are unlikely to be suitable for British appliances.

Cars

Where cars are not provided it may be worthwhile shipping a car abroad. Import duties on cars, both new and used, vary widely from country to country. It is wise to obtain details from the appropriate embassy some time before departure. Check, too, the prices of new and used cars in the new country. It may be cheaper to buy there. Another alternative is to buy a car for export which means it can be purchased within six months of leaving the UK and used here in the interim but neither VAT nor car tax will be charged so long as the car is exported within the six month period and is kept abroad (apart from UK visits) for a further 12 months. It is important to note that if the car is not exported, for whatever reason, tax becomes payable at the end of the six month period. Even if the car is stolen or wrecked and export is beyond the control of the owner, tax will be charged. Because of this possibility the car should be insured for its full value pending departure, not simply the tax free price.

Pets

There are animal moving specialists who can provide tailor-made travelling crates and interim boarding facilities if these are required, but much careful thought should be given to the question of pets abroad. Not only may they not take to the climatic change, they could be prey to disease, their presence may not be as acceptable in some countries as is the case in Britain, and on return they will face quarantine of six months at a cost of at least £2 per day. In general, pets are best left behind.

Planning the move

Planning an overseas move requires a good strategy to ensure minimum inconvenience and maximum efficiency. The following check list may prove helpful.

One month before your departure date you should:
- confirm the removal date with your contractor,
- dispose of all the things you are not taking abroad,
- draw up an inventory for customs (and keep two copies),
- evaluate your goods for insurance,
- find receipts for purchases which may be needed for customs clearance,
- make sure your passports are valid,
- supply the removal firm with a contact address, and
- check that they know your correct overseas address.

Three weeks before departure you should:
- check that your insurance policies have been paid for and implemented,
- arrange the settlement of accounts for services such as electricity and telephone,
- inform officials such as your bank manager, solicitor and accountant of your departure and arrange your overseas banking facilities,

- finalise arrangements for your pets,
- cancel any regular subscriptions, and
- arrange for the return of any rented equipment.

Two weeks before departure you should:
- locate all your official documents such as birth, marriage and medical certificates,
- arrange for your mail to be forwarded,
- check that there are no outstanding bills, and
- clean any garden implements ready for packing.

In the last week you should:
- check your own travel arrangements,
- check that any services that should be disconnected will be, and
- if you have children, arrange for them to be out of the way while the move is on.

On the penultimate day you should:
- confirm the time of arrival of the removers,
- ensure that you have to hand all documents, passports, tickets, etc.,
- put any personal items you want to travel with you quite separate,
- check that any services are disconnected, and
- check that you have the address and phone number of the contractor's agent overseas.

On the last day:
- relax and drain the gin bottle.

Settling in
Possibly one of the most important times in the life of the new expatriate is his first few hours in his new country. From his employer's point of view it is also one of the simplest to deal with, although it is often neglected. Having a company representative at the airport possibly to assist with immigration and customs clearance and certainly to drive the newcomer and his family to their destination can make an enormous difference to the expatriate's first impression of his new country.

On arriving in a new country it may often be best to stay at least the first night in a hotel unless the employer is one of the rare ones who actually takes the trouble to make sure that the accommodation is really ready for immediate occupation. This does not simply mean that the furniture is there but that the larder has been stocked and all the utilities are in working order.

In countries where there is a well-defined expatriate community the newcomer is unlikely to have any difficulty in getting to know his colleagues. By and large expatriates are a sociable and helpful bunch. For expatriate families it may be useful for the wife to contact the Women's Corona Society before leaving the UK. This expatriate women's organisation can provide briefings, background information and, most importantly, contacts in the new location and in some

21

countries the local Corona group will make a particular effort to help the newcomers settle in.

From this point it is entirely up to the expatriate himself what he makes of his overseas life. Inevitably, the first few weeks or months of a new expatriate posting are by far the most difficult. It is not unknown for people to pack up and leave after the first week or two because they cannot cope with the culture shock. This reaction should be avoidable by the expatriate doing his homework on his new country and the experience of many hundreds of expatriates with whom I have discussed this topic is that even if it seems intolerable in the first few weeks this does not last. In fact, I can think of only a handful of expatriates who have failed to enjoy their period overseas.

3

Taxation

UK TAXES: INCOME TAX

'Any income which belongs, or is deemed to belong, to a person resident in the UK is liable to UK income tax. Any income arising within the UK, whether it belongs to a resident or a non-resident, is also liable to UK income tax.' That statement of less than four dozen words forms the basis of the thousands of pages which have been written about UK income tax. What fills all these thousands of pages are definitions, exemptions, reliefs, deductions and procedures. Added to this basic structure is a network of tax avoidance devices which is usually followed by a new network of anti-avoidance legislation. All of this makes fertile ground for the tax consultant and nowhere more fruitful than in the field of expatriate taxation.

The expatriate needs to consider income tax before he leaves the UK, while he is abroad, and before he returns. Good personal taxation advice may not be cheap but it can be much cheaper than many of the mistakes which might otherwise be made. This taxation chapter as it relates to income tax and the other taxes provides the basic guidelines, and, with the chapter on investment and financial planning, will cover most of the situations encountered by most expatriates. Special rules apply to taxes concerning property and these are described in detail in the UK property chapter. If any particular situations or circumstances are not covered, then a letter to me will certainly elicit an explanation or further advice.

Definitions

Before going on to discuss the expatriate's actual tax liabilities it is important to grasp the full meaning of many of the terms used. Some items permit a brief and simple definition, others are much more complex. Thus a 'tax year' is the period from 6th April to the following 5th April; the UK comprises England, Scotland, Wales and Northern Ireland — it does not include either the Channel Islands or the Isle of Man (an important factor in the success of these islands as financial centres). The more important of the complex terms are described fully below.

Residence

The terms 'resident' and 'non-resident' are not defined anywhere in the tax legislation but, in tax cases involving the terms, they have been assumed to have their everyday meaning. What has to be decided is whether or not a person is resident in the UK for any particular tax year. Residence only ever refers to the position in a full tax year in the legislation but in certain circumstances (as described later) it may, by concession, relate to part of a year.

The flow chart on page 25 provides a guide to establishing residence status. However, it must be noted that charts of this nature are unlikely to be conclusive in every situation, and in complex cases it is essential to refer to a professional tax advisor. The flow chart in chapter 8 gives further guidance for the returning expatriate.

To be considered resident in the UK for tax purposes a person must be physically present in the UK for at least part of the year. In any year during which he is present in the UK for 183 days or more he will be considered resident. There are no exceptions to this rule. A person will also be regarded as resident in the UK if he visits the UK in four consecutive years and his annual visits average three months or more.

Finally, a person will be considered as UK resident in any year during which he makes any visit, however short, if he has accommodation available for his use. However, this need not concern the working expatriate greatly as availability of accommodation is ignored where a person is working full-time in a business or employment carried on wholly abroad. It will not be ignored, however, where the person owns a business or is a partner in one which is carried on mainly abroad but which has a branch or a permanent establishment in the UK. It is important too to note that the business or employment must be carried on wholly abroad barring mere incidentals. Incidental duties are highly restricted and include such things as reporting back to head office for further instructions, short periods of training, and other elements of a very minor nature. Non-incidental duties include attendance by directors at board meetings in the UK and, in the case of aircrew, more than a single landing and take off in the UK during the year (similar provisions apply to seafarers). Where more than incidental duties are performed in the UK then the expatriate can only obtain non-resident status if he has no accommodation available for his use in the UK. Whether or not accommodation is available is a question of fact; it does not require ownership nor, indeed, need the person actually use the accommodation during his visit. By the same token, ownership of accommodation does not necessarily mean it is available for use; the family home may be let on a long lease and entry forbidden to the owner.

It was noted above that residence is normally considered in the context of a complete tax year. There is one concessionary exception to this. The year may be split into a resident and a non-resident part in the following circumstances if the person:

(1) is a new permanent resident, provided that he has been not ordinarily resident in the UK; or
(2) has left the UK for permanent residence abroad, provided that he becomes not ordinarily resident in the UK; or
(3) subject to certain conditions, is taking full-time employment abroad.

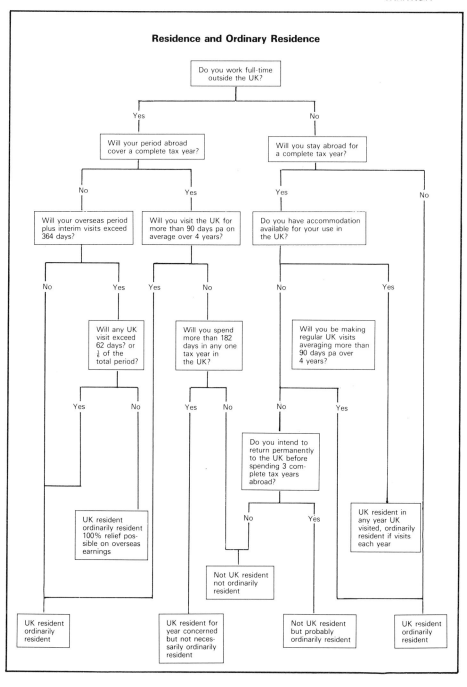

Residence and Ordinary Residence

Do you work full-time outside the UK?

Yes / No

Yes branch: Will your period abroad cover a complete tax year?

No / Yes

No: Will your overseas period plus interim visits exceed 364 days?

No / Yes

Yes (364 days): Will any UK visit exceed 62 days? or $\frac{1}{6}$ of the total period?

Yes / No

Yes branch (tax year): Will you visit the UK for more than 90 days pa on average over 4 years?

Yes / No

No (90 days): Will you spend more than 182 days in any one tax year in the UK?

Yes / No

No branch (main): Will you stay abroad for a complete tax year?

Yes / No

Yes: Do you have accommodation available for your use in the UK?

No / Yes

No (accommodation): Will you be making regular UK visits averaging more than 90 days pa over 4 years?

No / Yes

No (regular visits): Do you intend to return permanently to the UK before spending 3 complete tax years abroad?

No / Yes

Outcome boxes:

UK resident ordinarily resident 100% relief possible on overseas earnings

Not UK resident not ordinarily resident

UK resident in any year UK visited, ordinarily resident if visits each year

UK resident ordinarily resident

UK resident for year concerned but not necessarily ordinarily resident

Not UK resident but probably ordinarily resident

UK resident ordinarily resident

25

With 'Financial Adviser Offshore' you'll be the first to know when the tide turns.

Spotting undercurrents in offshore financial seas can be a risky business. So Financial Adviser, which has been such a success with brokers and investment consultants in Britain, has decided to start *Financial Adviser Offshore*.

And if you're a professional adviser you'll be able to receive it, air-speeded, every month, absolutely free.

Wherever you work, and whoever your clients, you can keep them up-to-date with the latest offshore investment opportunities. As well as news, features about new tax laws, offshore funds, and the best statistics service available.

Write to Ursula Zajac, Circulation manager, Financial Adviser, FT Business Information Ltd., 91-93 Charterhouse Street, London EC1M 6HR, on your business notepaper for a free subscription.

Where the year is split in this way the day of departure from, or arrival in, the UK falls into the period of residence in the UK. The working expatriate will be regarded as not resident and not ordinarily resident from the day following his departure until the day preceding his return subject to the following conditions:

(1)   that he goes abroad for full-time service under a contract of employment; and
(2)   that all the duties of the employment are carried on abroad other than mere incidental duties in the UK; and
(3)   that his absence from the UK in this employment spans at least one complete tax year; and
(4)   that interim visits to the UK do not amount to six months (183 days) or more in any one tax year or three months or more each year on average.

Ordinary residence
This is broadly equivalent to habitual residence; if a person is resident in the UK year after year he will be considered ordinarily resident in the UK. A person may be resident but not ordinarily resident in a particular year and, similarly, he can be ordinarily resident but not resident in a particular year. Ordinary residence is most relevant to investment income and capital gains.

Overruling the rules of residence and ordinary residence
Where the expatriate is living and working in a country with which the UK has a double taxation agreement, the UK rules relating to residence and ordinary residence (and the domestic rules of the other country) can be superceded by the rules contained in the double taxation agreement. Most tax treaties have specific provision for deciding the fiscal residence of affected individuals where there may be some conflict between the domestic law of the countries concerned. See later in this chapter and Appendix II.

Domicile
Unlike the terms 'resident' and 'ordinarily resident', 'domicile' is a concept of general law and is defined at length. Its main relevance to readers of this book will be in connection with inheritance tax and a detailed definition is given in that section. Domicile does have certain effects on income tax liability but for most British expatriates these are minor.

Income tax provisions
Most working expatriates, certainly those abroad full-time for more than two years, will have non-resident status and the obvious tax advantages this brings. Perhaps the simplest way to describe the various tax provisions appropriate to expatriates is to go through the three main stages one by one — tax in the year of departure, tax while abroad, and tax in the year of return.

Income tax in the year of departure
Prior to departure the vast majority of British expatriates will have been resident and ordinarily resident in the UK for tax purposes. But, as described above, the person will be considered as not resident and not ordinarily resident from the day following departure if he fulfils the conditions listed there. Where these conditions cannot be met, perhaps because the contract is for an indefinite period which may or may not include a full tax year, the Inland Revenue will not grant the non-resident status. In any event, non-resident status will be conditional until a full tax year has been spent outside the UK.

Where non-resident status can be granted, the intending expatriate may be able to claim a repayment of income tax already paid during the current tax year. This repayment may arise where the expatriate had been taxed under PAYE and is brought about by the manner in which personal allowances are granted in that system. Although UK resident for only part of the year, the intending expatriate will still be entitled to his full personal allowances. Under PAYE the allowances are given proportionately each week or month. Thus, by the end of September half of the allowance will have been given, by the end of December, three-quarters, and so on. The following example illustrates:

Mr Smith is paid £12,000pa and has a tax code of 300. This code means that he has personal allowances of about £3,000. Each month he will be given against his salary £250 of these allowances. Mr Smith takes up a new job abroad on 10th August 1987, which involves a three year contract full-time outside the UK. His final salary cheque from his UK employer is paid on 31st July. He can claim a tax rebate as follows:

UK income from 6th April 1987	= 4 × 1,000	=	£4,000
Personal allowances given	= 4 × 250	=	£1,000
Taxable income on which tax already paid			£3,000
Full allowances for the year	=	3,000	
Allowances given so far	=	1,000	
Balance of allowances due		2,000	2,000
Income taxable for the year			£1,000
Tax paid in 1987/88:	£3,000 @ 27%	=	£810
Tax due	£1,000 @ 27%	=	£270
Tax overpaid and to be rebated			£540

In that simple example there was no investment income to be considered. Where the individual's tax liability arises not only from wages or salary but includes investment income which is paid gross, such as National Savings Bank interest, or earnings from self-employment, the calculation will be different. Depending on the complexity of the case and the amounts of other income involved, the Revenue may defer making any repayment until after the end of the tax year

Where the extra income is small, the tax inspector may include an estimated amount in the repayment calculation and make an interim rebate. If, in the example above, Mr Smith had a National Savings Bank deposit, the interest on which was expected to be about £100, his tax inspector might estimate it at £150, the tax on which would be £40.50, and repay the balance of £499.50 to Mr Smith.

To claim this repayment of tax the expatriate should write to his tax office requesting form P85. At the same time he might usefully ask for Revenue Pamphlet IR20 entitled *Residents and Non-Residents Liability to Tax in the United Kingdom.*

The position of a wife who accompanies her husband overseas is rather more complex. If she was employed in the UK prior to departure she may be entitled to a tax rebate on the grounds that she has given up work for the balance of the tax year. In that case she can calculate her repayment in the same way as Mr Smith in the example given earlier. She cannot claim a rebate on the grounds that she will be non-resident after departure unless she, herself, fulfils all the conditions required. Where the wife herself has an overseas contract there will be no problem, but otherwise she will not be granted non-resident status for up to three years. Most expatriate wives in fact remain UK resident for tax purposes even when they spend as much time overseas as their husbands. This happens because most expatriate wives are not working full-time abroad and if they make any visit to the UK when accommodation is available for their use, whether it is actually used or not, they will be considered UK resident. This position can be altered by the provisions of a double taxation agreement. For the full-time working expatriate available accommodation in the UK is irrelevant; not so for the non-working wife. Unlike many other aspects of UK tax, husbands and wives are considered quite separately when it comes to residence and domicile. This can be used to advantage as described in the next section. One final point on spouses and accommodation: accommodation available to one spouse is deemed to be available to the other.

Income tax while abroad
To start with the bad news, where non-resident status has been granted provisionally and the expatriate returns permanently to the UK before he has served a full tax year abroad, then he will be considered as never having lost his resident status. This means that his worldwide income is liable to UK tax and this will include the value of all perks such as car and accommodation abroad. He may be entitled to exemption or relief on his overseas earnings and perks, but all of his investment income will be fully taxable. The Inland Revenue are totally immovable on this and the reasons for an early return do not concern them. The only time the tax authorities will not take action to obtain any tax due is if the taxpayer dies abroad before the completion of one tax year.

Where the possibility exists of an early return, perhaps because of political instability or health risks, the expatriate is well advised to consider a tax contingency insurance policy. These are described in chapter 5.

29

The happier situation arises when the expatriate becomes properly and officially non-resident. He will then have no UK income tax liability on any overseas income whether from earnings or overseas investments. It often happens that an expatriate is employed and paid by a British company in the UK. So long as his duties are performed wholly overseas his salary will be treated as earned from an overseas employment and will not be taxed. The exception to this is where the expatriate is a Crown Servant or a member of the British armed forces. For these people their pay remains taxable in the UK. This does not prevent them from obtaining non-resident status if they are abroad long enough and obey the visit rules. They may then benefit from tax free investment income on overseas securities and special overseas allowances will also be free from UK tax.

Where a UK tax liability remains is in connection with income arising in the UK. Strictly, UK source income is taxable in the UK unless it is exempted by statute, by concession or practice, or under the provisions of a double taxation convention. Statutorily exempt income of interest to the expatriate includes a foreign service allowance paid to Crown Servants as compensation for the extra cost of living abroad, and the interest paid on certain UK Government stocks where they are held by non-residents. These stocks are listed on page 66.

Income exempted by concession or practice is generally that income which would normally be paid gross in the UK and which might prove difficult for the Revenue to tax efficiently. Thus, for example, UK State pensions are generally paid gross to non-residents. Prior to 1985, when UK bank deposit interest was paid gross to depositors, this too was by concession not taxed. However, the 1984 Finance Act changed the rules for bank deposits whereby interest was paid to depositors net of tax where those depositors were UK resident. In the case of depositors who are not ordinarily UK resident and who sign a declaration to that effect, UK banks will pay gross interest. That said, the non-taxability of the interest remains concessionary. From April 1986 the same regime applies to deposits with UK building societies. As described in chapter 5 the expatriate may still be advised to keep his cash deposits offshore. In that way he ceases to rely on the Revenue concession on the taxability of UK interest and will be in a better tax position on his eventual return to the UK (see chapter 8). Other UK source income may be exempt from UK tax under a double taxation agreement between the UK and the country of residence.

Where income in the UK does not fall into any of the exempt categories it will be liable to UK income tax. Of greatest importance to most expatriates is income from property, dividends and other distributions from British stocks, shares and unit trusts. Income from property and the relevant tax provisions are described at length in chapter 6. At this point it is sufficient to say that income from UK property is always liable to UK tax. Dividends and other distributions are paid by British companies with an accompanying tax credit. The overall effect is that of receiving the dividend net of tax. Part of the tax credit may be repayable under a double tax agreement, otherwise it may be lost to the expatriate.

As a general rule non-residents are not entitled to any personal reliefs or allowances against their UK income. However, British subjects and certain other categories of people may be able to claim a proportion of these allowances. For most British working expatriates this proportional relief is unlikely to be of much benefit unless the UK income is substantial relative to total world income. Additionally, for the expatriate with UK bank or building society deposit interest, the concessionary treatment is withdrawn and the interest becomes taxable.

There does, however, appear to be an increasing number of British expatriates who are working abroad, perhaps in overseas armed forces, airlines and elsewhere, who have not insignificant UK pensions, for example. Also, with the ever increasing rental income available from UK properties some expatriates now have a greater proportion of their income arising in the UK than was the case a few years ago. For these people a claim for part of their UK tax allowance (a Section 27 claim) can be worthwhile.

Section 27 applies to all the following categories:

- British subjects or citizens of the Republic of Ireland,
- a person who is or has been in the service of the Crown, or who is employed in the service of any missionary society or in the service of a territory under Her Majesty's protection,
- anyone resident in the Isle of Man or Channel Islands,
- anyone who previously resided within the UK and is resident abroad for the sake of his or her health, or the health of a member of his or her family resident with him or her,
- a widow whose late husband was in the service of the Crown.

All personal reliefs are available to British expatriates but relief is restricted such that ''the income tax payable may not be reduced below an amount bearing the same proportion to the tax which would be payable on total income if it were all charged to UK tax as the income actually chargeable bears to the total income''. This somewhat convoluted provision is best illustrated by example.

Mr Alan is a hospital technician in Saudi Arabia; he is not resident and not ordinarily resident in the UK. Apart from his salary he has interest from bank deposits in the UK and in Jersey, plus rent from his UK property. He is married and accompanied by his wife in Saudi Arabia. Calculation of any relief available is shown below.

1987/88	Total income	UK income	UK tax deducted
Overseas salary	£15,000	—	—
Overseas bank interest	1,500	—	—
UK bank interest	500	500	—
UK rental income (net)	2,000	2,000	540
	£19,000	£2,500	£540
Less: personal allowance	3,795	3,795	
Taxable income	£15,205	—	
Tax liability	£4,105.35	Nil	

Relief under Section 27 must not reduce Mr Alan's tax liability below the following level:

$$£4,105.35 \times \frac{2,500}{19,000} = £540.18$$

In this case a claim under Section 27 is ineffective and no repayment can be made. The reason for this is that Mr Alan's bank deposit interest, although paid gross while he is not ordinarily resident, is nevertheless brought into charge on any claim to relief.

However, consider the situation with Mr James who has precisely the same total income as Mr Alan but who has no UK interest and whose overseas deposit interest is £2,000. The calculation proceeds as before but the minimum tax payable now is:

$$£4,105.35 \times \frac{2,000}{19,000} = £432.14$$

In this case Mr James can reclaim tax paid of £107.86. (Looked at in another way, if Mr Alan moved his UK cash deposits offshore he could have effectively increased his yield on those deposits by some 21.6% — a powerful argument for not banking in the UK.)

For the more highly paid expatriates, certainly those earning £25,000 per annum or more, an annual Section 27 claim is unlikely to produce a significant repayment unless UK income is very high. However, claims can be made up to six years in arrears and if the expatriate can face up to all the arithmetic involved a claim for several years together might be somewhat more cost-effective. For those wishing to make such a claim the necessary forms can be obtained from Inland Revenue, Claims Branch, Magdalin House, Stanley Precinct, Bootle, Liverpool L69 9BB.

Another way in which expatriates with UK taxable income can reduce the Revenue's depredations is by making use of Deeds of Covenant. Covenants are commonly used by UK residents to provide adult children with funds at university or further education. Covenants to minor children are ineffective in that income derived from a parental source is treated as the parents' income until such time as the child is 18 or marries, if sooner. This is not the case where the parent is not resident for tax purposes. In this case the income would be treated as the income of the child and since all children are entitled to a personal allowance in their own right, this allowance can be used to reclaim any tax deducted by the parent in paying the covenanted sum. Many expatriates have found this particularly useful in paying for school fees, for example. The following illustration shows the potential worth of such a scheme. (It should be noted, however, that there are now signs that the Inland Revenue may challenge these arrangements.):

Captain Smith is employed by an overseas airline and he has an RAF pension of £2,000 per annum. A Section 27 claim is inapplicable as he has very little other UK income and his overseas salary is in excess of £50,000. In consequence, he pays £540 per annum tax on his pension. His 12 year-old daughter is at boarding school in the UK and his personal liability for her school fees amounts to some £2,800 per annum. By making a Deed of Covenant in his daughter's favour for £2,000 (gross) per annum he can make use of the tax deducted from his pension to reduce the cost of school fees. He makes a net payment to his daughter of £1,460, at the end of the tax year his daughter (or her guardian) makes a claim for repayment of tax deducted at source and since her income is below the single person's allowance (£2,425 in 1987/88) all tax deducted will be repaid to her.

The Inland Revenue themselves provide forms of Deeds of Covenant for children undergoing further education and the wording on these forms can be adapted to suit younger children. However, the following wording has so far proved acceptable to the Inland Revenue and can be adjusted as required by the individual expatriate.

I, . . . (NAME) . . . . of . . . .

. . . (ADDRESS) . . . . covenant to pay

. . . (CHILD'S NAME) . . . . of . . . (CHILD'S . .

. . . ADDRESS) . . . . . . a gross amount of £ . . . . a year each a year for a period of (*) years, or for the period of our joint lives, or until . . . (HE/SHE) . . . ceases to be receiving full-time education at any school, college, university or any other educational establishment (whichever is the shorter period), the first payment to be made on . . . (DATE) . . .

Dated . . . .

Signed, sealed and delivered by . . . .

. . . .   Seal

In the presence of . . . .

Name of witness   . . . .

Address of witness . . . .

. . . .

. . . .

*Commonly the number of years to the end of schooling, etc, but in any event, at least 7 years.

Finally, it should be noted that it is not even essential that the child is UK resident because if he or she has no other income and qualifies under the headings given earlier for Section 27 relief then all tax can be repaid up to the amount of the personal allowance. It should be further noted, however, that a Deed of Covenant signed, sealed and delivered outside the UK is ineffective for UK tax so such legalities should be conducted in the UK.

It has already been mentioned that most expatriate wives remain technically resident for UK tax purposes. This can, in certain circumstances, be turned to advantage. If for a tax year a married woman is living with her husband but one of them is resident in the UK either for part or the whole of the year and the other is not resident for the year, they are regarded for income tax purposes as if they were permanently separated, and entitled to make separate claims, if it is to their advantage, i.e. the wife may claim to be treated as a single person. This means that instead of being entitled to the wife's earned income allowance, which as its terminology implies is an allowance available only against earned income, she is entitled to the normal single person's allowance which can be used to offset earned or investment income. This situation can be utilised, for example, where the wife receives the rental income on the family home. Similarly she can reclaim the tax credit which accompanies UK company dividends or any other income which is received net on which tax deducted at source can be reclaimed (note that bank and building society deposits should not be in the wife's name as tax deducted therefrom cannot be reclaimed under any circumstances — deposits held by non-residents can, of course, be paid gross). A further advantage accrues to a "resident" wife who is also the mother of minor children. If she has care and control of those children, which would normally be the case, then she may also claim the additional personal allowance which gives her a total allowance equivalent to that of a married man in the UK. In this way gross investment income equal to £3,795 payable to a "resident" wife in 1987/88 would be tax free, or, looked at another way, up to £1,024.65 tax deducted at source can be reclaimed by a wife in these circumstances. A simple example illustrates the case:

Mr and Mrs Jones own two properties in the UK — their family home in Cambridge and a holiday cottage in Norfolk. The family home is rented out and they use the Norfolk cottage for their annual home leaves. In addition to their rental income they also receive dividends from a portfolio of UK shares and unit trusts. If they make no attempt to make use of Mrs Jones's UK residency then their situation is as follows:

	Income	Tax payable or deducted
Rent (net of expenses)	£2,000	£540
Dividends	1,095	—
Tax credit	405	405
	£3,500	£945
Total net income	£2,555	

However, if the rent was receivable by Mrs Jones and the dividends were payable to her (involving a change from perhaps Mr Jones' or joint ownership) the total amount of tax can be relieved (Mrs Jones' children are at school in the UK).

Total income		£3,500
Personal allowance	£2,425	
Additional personal allowance	£1,370	£3,795
Taxable income		Nil
Total net income		£3,500

All tax deducted to be repaid

The situation can be quite different, however, where the wife perhaps remains in the UK and is earning a salary well in excess of her personal allowance and where any additional income would be taxable, possibly even at higher rates. Under these circumstances it is important that the UK source investment income, be it from dividends or rent or whatever, is in the name of the husband. In this way, unless the income is itself very substantial, ie over £17,900 at least, only basic rate tax will be payable by the husband. Where bank deposits are concerned it is also obviously in the family's interest (for tax reasons at least) that these accounts should be in the name of the non-resident. Where investments are held jointly and the wife is taxable then she may well be taxed as her husband's resident agent and they could lose the exempt treatment given to, for example, bank and building society deposits.

Another advantage which was enjoyed by the resident/non-resident couple concerned life assurance relief. This relief was given in the UK by means of net premiums, that is if the premium for a particular life policy was £100 the actual premium paid by the policyholder was £85. The 15 per cent tax relief was claimed from the Inland Revenue by the life assurance company. But after the end of the year of departure the non-resident was not entitled to this relief, he had to inform the company and revert to paying the full, gross, premium. However, tax relief was available to the payer of the premiums whether the policy was on the payer's life or on the life of his or her spouse. Thus, if the resident wife took out a policy on her non-resident husband, she could obtain the tax relief. Following the abolition of life assurance relief on new policies in 1984 this advantage has obviously been lost, but it is well worth checking pre-1984 policies to make sure that any relief available has, in fact, been given.

Taxation in the year of return
In terms of tax planning this is one of the most important and complex periods. Planning must be initiated some time before return if expensive mistakes are to be avoided. The main problem areas do not involve earnings but are concerned primarily with investment income and capital gains. Detailed advice on both tax and investments at this time is given in chapter 8 — **Returning home**.

The business traveller and the semi-expatriate

So far in this chapter I have been concerned only with the expatriate who achieves non-resident status. Many people, however, work for long periods abroad without ever losing their status as UK resident. Consider the situations of Mr Brown and Mr Black:

Mr Brown leaves the UK to work in Nigeria. He leaves on 1st April 1985 and returns on 1st May 1986. He has been abroad 13 months and because he has been away for a complete tax year he would be considered non-resident from 1st April 1985 until 30th April 1986. Mr Black, on the other hand, followed Mr Brown to Nigeria two weeks later, on 15th April 1985. He stayed on after Mr Brown returned and eventually came home himself on 15th March 1987. Mr Black has been abroad for 23 months but because he has not been away over a complete tax year, he will have remained UK resident throughout.

Then there is Mr Green. He rarely leaves the UK for more than a month at a time but he regularly spends a total of eight or nine months each year overseas. He, like Mr Black, remains UK resident throughout.

Of the Messrs Brown, Black and Green, Mr Brown has the obvious advantage in that he can achieve the tax free status of non-resident. But Mr Black may not do too badly; he may qualify for 100 per cent exemption from tax on his overseas earnings. Unfortunately, these days Mr Green is entitled to no relief whatsoever. Up to 1983/84 he could benefit from 25 per cent exemption on his earnings from the overseas work and for 1984/85 a reduced relief of 12½ per cent exemption. The relief was totally withdrawn for tax years 1985/86 onwards. However, for readers who have been in this position and who have not claimed or been given their relief, there is a period of six years after the particular year of assessment concerned during which they may still claim. The last date for claims relating to 1984/85 is therefore 5th April 1991.

100 per cent exemption — the '365 day rule'

In 1977 the then Chancellor of the Exchequer, Denis Healey, intro-duced certain tax reliefs for those people he described as being 'at the sharp end of exporting'. The reliefs were intended for those who were not abroad long enough at any time to become non-resident but who spent, nonetheless, a significant period abroad. The most important of these reliefs is that available to the person who works abroad but whose overseas service does not span a complete tax year, although it does last for more than twelve months. Such people can be regarded as 'semi-expatriates'. Relief is given by total exemption from UK tax of all income relating to the work done abroad. To qualify for this relief a person has to show that he worked abroad for a 'qualifying period' of at least 365 days. This period is not confined to one particular tax year and almost invariably will span two or more tax years. The legis-lation relating to this relief is complex and is most easily explained by examples or mathematical formulae. Both are used below. What the semi-expatriate must remember above all is to keep a close watch on his UK visits.

A 'qualifying period' comprises either consecutive days of absence from the UK or periods of absence plus intervening periods in the UK provided that the intervening periods satisfy the following conditions:

(1)   no period spent in the UK exceeds 62 consecutive days, and
(2)   the total number of intervening days in the UK is less than 1/6th of the total number of days in the period under consideration.

For example, Mr White travels extensively for his company and his movements are as follows:

Period	Days outside the UK	Days in the UK	Cumulative total	
A	50	—	50	
B	—	10	60	
C	120	—	180	1/6th = 30
D	—	25	205	
E	161	—	366	1/6th = 61
F	—	45	411	
G	63	—	474	1/6th = 79
H	—	1		
I	280	—		
J	—	20		
K	2	—		

Periods A, C, E, G, I and K are all qualifying periods because they are days of absence from the UK. None, of themselves, give rise to any tax advantage since they do not individually last for 365 days. Period A-C is also a qualifying period; so too is period A-E. Because the latter is greater than 365 days it does confer a tax advantage. In that period no visit lasted longer than 62 days and the total time spent in the UK is less than 1/6th of the total period. Period A-G is not a qualifying period because days spent in the UK (80) exceed 1/6th of the total period. Had one day less been spent in the UK during the last visit or had a few more days been spent abroad, then the whole period might have been a qualifying period. In the example, however, there is a new qualifying period which will again give tax relief — period G-K. In summary, income earned during the period A-E will be tax exempt, income earned during period F will be taxable, and income earned during period G-K will be exempt.

For readers with a bent towards mathematics or logic the rules can be expressed in those terms much more succinctly than they appear in the legislation, and the resulting formulae may be used for an easy check on when visits can be made and how long such visits can last. Using simple notation the formulae are produced as shown overleaf.

Days spent abroad	Days spent in the UK
a_1	
—	b_1
a_2	—
—	b_2
a_3	—
—	b_3
a_4	—

For the period from the beginning of a_1 to the end of a_2 to be a qualifying period, b_1 must be less than $1/6(a_1 + a_2 + b_1)$. Similarly, for the period from a_1 to a_3 to qualify, $b_1 + b_2$ must be less than $1/6(a_1 + a_2 + a_3 + b_1 + b_2)$, and so on throughout the total period. Where the total period exceeds 365 days then the tax exemption will apply. Using the above notation, the rules may be stated thus:

$$\text{Qualifying period: } \sum_1^{n+1} a_n + \sum_1^n b_n \geqslant 365$$

$$\text{UK visits: } b_n \leqslant 62$$

$$\text{Total UK visits: } \sum_1^n b_n \leqslant \frac{1}{6}\left(\sum_1^{n+1} a_n + \sum_1^n b_n \right)$$

From these formulae it is fairly straightforward to keep a check on UK visits and when they can next be made. At the end of a visit lasting no more than 62 days the length of time which must be spent abroad before the next visit can be calculated from the formula

$$a_z \geqslant 5 \sum_1^n b_n - \sum_1^n a_n \quad \text{where } a_z \text{ is the time to be spent abroad.}$$

The following example illustrates the minimum overseas periods after the initial spell and the first visit.

Days abroad a_n	Days in the UK b_n	Total $a_n + b_n$	Minimum abroad before next visit $6b_n - (a_n + b_n)$ $= 5\sum b_n - \sum a_n$
100	—	100	
—	28	128	40
40	—	168	
—	21	189	105
105	—	294	
—	28	322	140
140	—	362	

After the last period of 140 days the qualifying period is of sufficient length to give tax exemption.

Going on from this to a further refinement, the permitted length of any proposed UK visit can be calculated provided an assumption is made about the length of the subsequent period to be spent abroad. In the following example it is assumed that the next period to be spent abroad will be at least five weeks:

Days abroad	Days in the UK
60	—
—	10
40	—
—	30
100	—
—	14
80	—
—	y
35	—
Total 315	54 + y

$$54 + y \leqslant 1/6(315 + (54 + y))$$
$$y \leqslant 1/6(315 + (54 + y)) - 54$$
$$6y \leqslant 315 + 54 + y - 324$$
$$y \leqslant 1/5(45)$$
$$\leqslant 9$$

Thus the maximum length of the contemplated visit is nine days. Where z is the number of days still to be spent abroad, or the minimum guaranteed duration of the next spell abroad, then with the a and b notation used previously the permitted length of any visit may be expressed thus:

$$b_{n+1} \leqslant \frac{1}{6} \left(\sum_{1}^{n} a_n + z \right) - \sum_{1}^{n} b_n$$

Returning from the realms of advanced mathematics it may be worth repeating that the 100 per cent relief is complex but if visits are carefully monitored it should present little problem.

An important point to bear in mind for 100 per cent relief is the initial and end timing of the qualifying period. Consider the case of Mr John and Mr James; both go abroad for 18 months, both are paid £1,000 per month before they go and on their return; both are entitled to tax allowances totalling £3,000. Mr John goes abroad on 1st July 1986 and returns on 31st December 1987; Mr James goes abroad on 1st May 1986 and returns on 31st October 1987. Their UK tax positions for years 1986/87 and 1987/88 are given overleaf (both have complete exemption of earnings while abroad):

Mr John

1986/87	Income: 3 months @ £1,000	=	£3,000
	Allowances		£3,000
	Taxable income		NIL
1987/88	Income: 3 months @ £1,000	=	£3,000
	Allowances		£3,000
	Taxable income		NIL

Mr James

1986/87	Income: 1 month @ £1,000	=	£1,000
	Allowances		£3,000
	Taxable income		NIL
1987/88	Income: 5 months @ £1,000	=	£5,000
	Allowances		£3,000
	Taxable income		£2,000
	Tax payable @ 27%	=	£540

Wherever possible the business traveller should try to obtain maximum advantage from his tax allowances. In the example above Mr James lost most of his although, if his wife had income, the balance could be used there.

Two final points might usefully be borne in mind regarding this relief. The first concerns the amount of time actually spent working abroad: the legislation refers to overseas work 'in the course of a qualifying period' — there does not appear to be a requirement that the employment itself should last for the whole of that period. Thus, an absence of 365 days made up of six months work and six months overseas holiday could still be a qualifying period. This is an extreme case which, to my knowledge, has not been tested in the courts but it is certainly accepted that a more modest level of holiday spent abroad will be considered as part of the overseas portion in a qualifying period. Similarly, a period of terminal leave spent outside the UK will also qualify for exemption. Holiday pay or terminal gratuities applicable to a spell of overseas working which has spanned a 365-day qualifying period will themselves qualify for exemption even if the holiday is spent in the UK or if the payment is received after return to the UK. Finally, there is a word of warning. The earnings which qualify for relief are those which are attributable to the period of overseas work. Someone who works solely abroad can therefore have exemption of all his earned income, but someone who works partly abroad and partly in the UK (where the UK duties are more than merely incidental) could have his emoluments apportioned and relief given only on the overseas portion. Inland Revenue practice, however, is to permit relief on the whole of the earnings unless there is an appearance of artificiality about the employee's arrangements with the employer. Suspicion is often engendered where there are two or more associated employments and great care must be exercised with these even where there is a bona fide reason for such an arrangement.

Where 100 per cent exemption applies it covers all emoluments — salary, bonuses and allowances, and benefits in kind. Given the total taxable value of all of these in the UK for a typical expatriate package, the need and the incentive for keeping a careful eye on UK visits is apparent. A not untypical expatriate remuneration package might be made up as follows:

Salary	£30,000 pa
Travel benefit	8,000
Housing benefit	15,000
Servants, etc	10,000
Cars, etc	3,000
School fees, etc	5,000
Medical insurance	1,000
Bonus	10,000
	£82,000

If UK taxable, tax payable = £38,581

In this case the penalty for not obeying the rules would be a tax bill equivalent to almost the total direct income payment.

25 per cent relief and the '30 day rule' (12½ per cent for 1984/85)
As mentioned above this relief has been phased out. However, it may be important for readers who have been entitled to make a claim under this rule to have the details available at least until 1991.

To come into this category a person must be either an employee of a UK resident company or self-employed and spend a minimum of 30 'qualifying days' outside the UK in any one tax year. A 'qualifying day' is a day of absence from the UK (that is, absent at the end of the day — midnight) and one which meets one or other of the following criteria:

(1) it is substantially devoted to the performance outside the UK of one or more employments or, in the case of the self-employed, is substantially devoted to the business; or
(2) it is one of at least seven consecutive days of absence which, taken as a whole, are substantially devoted to the duties of the employment or to the business; or
(3) it is spent travelling for the purposes of the employment or the business.

Assuming these conditions are met then the person is entitled to tax relief. However, as in other aspects of UK tax, employees and the self-employed are treated differently.

For the employee the minimum relief available is exemption from tax of 25 (12½) per cent of the earnings relating to the overseas work as calculated on a time-apportionment basis; that is, the number of qualifying days divided by 365 multiplied by earnings for the year. For example, Mr Gray spends 50 qualifying days outside the UK in 1983/84. His annual salary is £15,000. The tax-exempt amount is:

$$25\% \times 50/365 \times £15,000 = £514$$

41

For the basic rate taxpayer this represents a tax saving of £154. But there may be more. The legislation allows the relief to exceed the basic time-apportioned amount in order to properly reflect what is reasonable with regard to the nature of, and the time actually devoted to, the work abroad compared to that at home. A more detailed look at Mr Gray's position will illustrate. The second qualifying day criterion described above implies that weekends or other days off might be included in absences of a week or more. Suppose Mr Gray's 50 qualifying days did not include any weekends, holidays, or days off. It would, in those circumstances, appear just and reasonable to reduce the denominator to the number of days normally worked in the year, say 260. Suppose further that instead of a normal eight hour day Mr Gray works for twelve hours each day he is abroad — not unusual with meetings and conferences running into the evening. It would then appear just and reasonable to uprate the number of qualifying days by a further 50 per cent. The result of these suppositions is to take the fraction from its original 50/365 to 50/260 to 75/285. Finally, suppose the corresponding salary for Mr Gray's job overseas (in the country or countries in which he operates) is 50 per cent higher than the £15,000 he receives. This could lead to a further enhancement of the fraction to $(75 + 37.5) \div (285 + 37.5)$, that is, $122.5 \div 322.5$. Applying this fraction to his annual earnings times 25 per cent, Mr Gray's tax saving increases from £154 to £392.

It must be said that the Inland Revenue is most reluctant to go beyond the minimum relief and would doubtless throw up its collective hands in horror at a claim along the lines of Mr Gray's second attempt. However, any reasonable case for using some of the uprating devices should be pursued. Success in the battle for an uprating of the emoluments relieved can often come down to the tactics employed. A logical statement as illustrated above to reduce the denominator may well result in a dusty reply along the lines of the legislation not making any allowance for any fraction other than 365ths. This is mere obfuscation and should not be accepted. It is merely a means of arriving at a fair measure of relievable income; the fact that it is expressed as a fraction is a coincidental convenience. That said, a test of reasonableness is always worth applying in any claim that may prove to be contentious. In any event the Inland Revenue have accepted a case for uplifting the relievable emoluments in at least one situation: a 50 per cent uplift is allowed automatically to certain airline pilots and other aircrew. The rationale behind this is that most aircrew are entitled to one day off for every two days spent flying away from their base. The uplift is granted by increasing the prescribed proportion by one day for every two qualifying days actually achieved. (Thirty qualifying days must still be actually achieved before any allowance is due.)

In any case the business traveller must first make a claim for relief and he must be able to justify it precisely. In straightforward basic relief claims, exemption in subsequent years will normally be obtained via the employer's PAYE scheme. Depending on how complex a claim the individual wishes to make, and depending on how rigorous his tax inspector is, he should retain all evidence of his trips. The minimum requirement is ticket stubs showing dates of departure and return. Employer's records, business appointment diaries and even passports can all be used to substantiate a claim.

What can be of particular assistance in obtaining the maximum tax relief is to obtain a form of separate agreement relating to overseas work, perhaps a special overseas bonus or commission structure or simply a higher hourly rate for the job. It is, however, very important that such an arrangement cannot be challenged as artificial or purely intended to confer an unreasonable tax advantage. The test of reasonableness again applies.

For the self-employed, relief is in some respects simpler than for employees but it does offer more scope for tax planning. The relief is given by reducing the profit for a year of assessment (after deducting capital allowances and stock relief) by $x/365 \times 25\%$ where x is the number of qualifying days. There is no scope for uprating this fraction. The tax planning angle comes from the basis of assessment for self-employed earnings — the previous year basis. For example, Mr Dark makes up his annual accounts to 31st December 1982. The profits for that year are assessed in 1983/84 with tax payable on 1st January and 1st July 1984. Tax relief for overseas work, however, is based on the time spent abroad during the year of assessment — 1983/84 — rather than in the year when the profits were actually made. Thus, if large profits were made by Mr Dark in the year to 31st December 1982 he can obtain substantial relief by increasing his foreign travel for business purposes in the tax year 1983/84.

But a word of warning: before Mr Dark boards the plane for Saudi Arabia he must ensure that his overseas relief does not clash with other relief which might be available for such items as capital expenditure. For the self-employed, good professional advice is essential.

25 per cent relief and foreign employments (12½ per cent for 1984/85)
In this final category, exemption from tax may be claimed on 25 per cent of earnings in respect of overseas employment if it is with a non-resident employer and the duties of the employment are performed wholly abroad. There is no minimum time requirement and no 30-day rule.

For example, Mr Light is a director of Alpha plc, a UK company, and also of Beta GmbH in Germany. The two companies are not connected. The German employment requires Mr Light to work in Germany for 20 days each year and none of his work for Beta is carried out in the UK. His German directorship pays DM10,000pa. The amount exempt from UK tax is the sterling equivalent of DM2,500.

If, however, the two employments were connected, Beta GmbH being a subsidiary of Alpha plc, vice versa, or both being subsidiaries of Gamma Inc., there might be problems. In such a case the Inland Revenue will seek to impose a time apportionment on all the overseas business. It will then be up to the individual to prove that, even if the employments are associated, the German remuneration was the appropriate rate for the job and not simply a tax avoidance device.

43

Expenses and benefits in kind

Apart from the tax exemptions described above the semi-expatriate or the travelling businessman can obtain further relief on essential expenditure. Travelling expenses deductible (or not charged to tax if reimbursed by an employer) are those which are necessarily incurred in the performance of the duties of the employment. Normally the cost of associated hotel expenses, etc. when travelling away from home will also be allowed.

Where an employee is overseas for a continuous period of at least 60 days then the payment or reimbursement by the employer of certain other expenses is allowed tax free. These are:

(1)   any accompanying journey at the beginning of the period, or an interim visit by the employee's spouse or children under 18;
(2)   any visit by him at the end of that period to visit his spouse or his children; and
(3)   any return journey following either of the former.

The exemption applies to up to two return journeys by the same person in a tax year and is only available where the employer foots the bill, so if the employee pays it all himself and is not reimbursed by the employer he cannot claim the deduction against his own tax. The cost of dependants' board and lodging is not included in the relief. These reliefs are not altered by the Finance Act 1984.

UK TAXES — CAPITAL GAINS TAX

Capital gains tax is assessed where there is a profitable or notionally profitable disposal of a chargeable asset by a person resident or ordinarily resident in the UK. The terms 'resident' and 'ordinarily resident' have been explained in the preceding section on income tax. CGT can be payable on chargeable disposals in a tax year if the individual is resident or ordinarily resident in the UK for any part of that year. However, by concession, the Revenue will not seek to tax gains made after the date on which a person becomes non-resident and not ordinarily resident. Similarly, a person making chargeable gains in the same tax year as his return to the UK but before he actually returns may also be liable to CGT. But where he has been abroad for at least 36 months this provision will not apply.

The general rules regarding CGT and expatriates can be simply stated:
(1)   delay making any profitable disposals until after departure from the UK;
(2)   make disposals showing losses before leaving the UK (the losses can then be carried forward to later years when the expatriate has again become UK resident and may be used to offset gains arising at that time);
(3)   make any profitable disposals before returning to the UK (in the tax year prior to the year of return if the overseas stay is less than 36 months);

44

(4) delay making any disposals showing losses until after return to the UK.

Note: The date of disposal for a property is the day on which the contract becomes unconditional not when completion takes place.

These rules are shown in chart form for returning expatriates on page 122.

These rules, of course, take into account only capital gains tax in the UK. Other countries also tax capital gains and it is important that the expatriate checks what his liability there might be before making any disposals either before or after leaving the UK. Leaving the UK frying pan for the overseas fire has little to recommend it.

Exemptions
Not all disposals give rise to chargeable gains in the UK. Certain assets are exempt as are certain disposals. The most important of these for the expatriate are described below.

Exempt assets
The largest single asset most of us have, the family home, is exempt from CGT on disposal. There are several special conditions relating to this 'principal private residence' exemption and these are described in chapter 6 — **UK property**. The other major exemption relates to Government stocks which are exempt if they are held for more than twelve months before disposal. Similar relief has been granted under the Finance Act 1984 to corporate loan stock.

Exempt disposals
Disposals between spouses who are living together do not give rise to capital gains or losses. The receiving spouse is deemed to have acquired the asset at its original cost to the other spouse. Where one spouse is resident and the other is non-resident, they are not considered as living together. An expatriate couple can take advantage of the spouse rules to make some disposals which might otherwise be taxable. If, for example, Mr and Mrs Evans are going abroad for a few years, Mr Evans will be non-resident but Mrs Evans remains UK resident and she has an investment portfolio showing substantial gains. Were she to sell she would be liable for CGT, but if she transfers it to her husband while both are UK resident, i.e. before they leave the UK, he can then sell after leaving without any CGT liability. Transfer to a non-resident spouse can also be treated in the same way but it must be noted that such a transaction is perhaps more likely to be attacked by the Inland Revenue as a wholly artificial transaction designed simply to achieve a tax advantage and under the tax case *Furniss v. Dawson* the results of such a transaction can be set aside. Other exempt disposals include gifts to charities and certain national institutions. (Other gifts of chargeable assets will be deemed to be made at market value and any notional gain may be assessed.) The deemed disposal of assets at death is not charged and any beneficiaries of chargeable assets will be deemed to have received them at their market value at the date of death.

Capital gains tax rates

Where capital gains tax is chargeable, it is at a flat rate of 30 per cent and for 1987/88 the first £6,600 of gains are tax free. This tax free limit will be uprated each year to take account of inflation. From 1982/83 the acquisition cost of chargeable assets is also adjusted in line with the retail price index so that purely inflationary gains accruing after 1982/83 are not taxed in the future.

As with income tax, capital gains tax requires consideration before returning to the UK. These points are discussed in chapter 8.

UK TAXES — INHERITANCE TAX

Unlike income tax and capital gains tax, inheritance tax is not normally concerned with the concepts of residence or ordinary residence. Potential liability for inheritance tax (IHT) is determined by two criteria — the domicile of the individual and the location of assets. Any UK domiciled person has a potential IHT liability no matter where in the world his assets are located. A non-UK domiciled person has a potential IHT liability if he has assets situated in the UK.

Inheritance tax replaced capital transfer tax in 1986. Capital transfer tax itself replaced estate duty in 1974. The IHT rules are very much those of capital transfer tax (CTT) but with several important qualifications. Before describing the tax in detail the essential term — domicile — should be fully understood.

Domicile

Domicile is not an easy concept to understand. You will look in vain for a definition in the Taxes Acts and you will find that in the case of inheritance tax it is given an artificially extended meaning involving a "deemed domicile" (see later). Although it is of relatively little importance for tax considerations, it should be noted that technically there is no such thing as a UK domicile. A person will be domiciled in Scotland, England (and Wales) or Northern Ireland. However for present purposes I shall use the terms UK or non-UK domicile. A person can and may only have one domicile at any one time (in contrast to residence where a person may be resident in two or more countries — or none — for tax purposes in the same tax year). Domicile basically exists in three forms — domicile of origin, domicile of dependence and domicile of choice.

A person acquires a domicile of origin at birth from the person upon whom he is legally dependent at that time irrespective of where he is born. Where the child's parents are married the domicile acquired is that of the father. Where they are unmarried the domicile is that of the mother. This domicile of origin is presumed to continue unless and until some event changes it. A change to a new domicile may be either to a new domicile of dependency or to a domicile of choice. A domicile of dependency normally arises in one of two ways. Where the individual concerned is under 16 years of age (14 for males and 12 for females in Scotland) and his parents change their domicile, then the child will acquire their new domicile of choice as his domicile of dependency. The second aspect of domicile of dependency relates to women who married before 1974. Up until 1st January 1974 a married woman automatically acquired the domicile of her husband. Since that time a married woman's domicile is determined in the same way as that of any other individual who is capable of having an independent domicile. This change was not retrospective and any woman already married on 1st January 1974 retains her existing domicile, ie that of her husband, until such time as she changes it by specific action.

Domicile of choice is perhaps the most important form of domicile for expatriates and certainly those contemplating retiring abroad. Changing an existing domicile of origin or dependency to a new domicile of choice is not always easy. The Inland Revenue will resist accepting a change from an established UK domicile to a new foreign domicile unless the individual can produce satisfactory evidence of his long term intentions and show that his purported change of domicile is permanent. Basically, a person's independent domicile is established by his intention to reside permanently in that country. Understandably, proving intent or permanence is somewhat difficult. There are, however, certain facts which may point to a new domicile of choice. Commonly these will include the following:

● residence in the new country,
● purchase of property there,
● disposal of property in the old country,
● development of business, social, religious and political interests in the new country,
● burial arrangements in the new country,
● where children are involved, their education locally in the new country,
● wills written under the laws of the new country,
● citizenship of the new country,
● so far as possible severance of all ties with the old country.

Domicile should not be confused with citizenship, nationality, or even a long term stay in a country other than one's own. These aspects remain only pointers to the legal domicile. A common problem for married couples who retire overseas and who have complied with all the pointers listed above arises on the death of one spouse. The survivor may prefer not to stay overseas but to return to the UK or go elsewhere, perhaps to be close to other members of his or her family. This abandonment of a domicile of choice can have an unfortunate tax effect. Where a domicile of choice is abandoned then the domicile of origin revises until such time as a new domicile of choice is acquired. It would be open to the authorities to claim that because the domicile of choice was abandoned, the required permanent intent had not existed and that the original domicile prevailed throughout. Any such suggestion should, however, be vigorously resisted. Conversely, the Inland Revenue, liking as they do to both have their cake and eat it, apply somewhat different strictures to non-UK domiciled individuals coming to the UK. In these cases the Revenue assumption is that such individuals are exercising their right to change to a new domicile of choice, ie the UK, with all the tax implications that this has. Such people can, in certain circumstances, enjoy very significant income tax and capital gains tax benefits by retaining a non-UK domicile. These however are beyond the scope of this book and are of little relevance to the majority of British expatriates.

As has already been mentioned, domicile is given an extended meaning for inheritance tax purposes whereby a person is treated as domiciled in the United Kingdom if,

(a) he was domiciled in the UK on or after 10th December 1974 and within the three years immediately preceding the relevant time; or

(b) he was resident in the UK on or after 10th December 1974, and in at least 17 our of 20 income tax years, ending with the income tax year in which the relevant time falls.

The relevant time is the occasion of any charge to inheritance tax. Briefly what this means is that even where a person has changed his domicile from the UK to a foreign domicile, his potential liability for inheritance tax continues unchanged for three years. In the case of long term British residents who are not domiciled here, there must be an absence of three complete income tax years before they can be free of inheritance tax.

The flow chart on page 49 gives a simplified route for deciding your domicile.

The tax itself

The name "inheritance tax" while not wholly a misnomer does not tell the entire story. Its predecessor, capital transfer tax, was precisely what its name implied — a tax on the transfer of capital either by way of gift or bequest. Inheritance tax is payable not only on bequests, albeit that is where the major liability is likely to arise, but in certain circumstances on the transfer of lifetime gifts, particularly gifts into settlement.

In March 1986 when CTT was transmogrified to IHT the new tax looked much simpler and appeared to confer many major advantages on potential taxpayers. Lifetime gifts between individuals became exempt (so long as the donor survived for seven years after the gift), non-exempt transfers would only be accumulated over a seven year period (compared to ten years with CTT, and prior to 1981 over the transferror's lifetime under CTT), and transfers into trusts would attract only 50 per cent of the IHT tax rate. But, as usual, nothing is as simple as it appears in the tax world. But that said, the 1987 Finance Act has brought further simplification into the IHT regime and an outline of the current position is provided below.

Briefly, where an individual makes a gift or a capital transfer to another individual then that transfer is potentially exempt. Where the transferror survives for seven years no tax is payable but should he die within that period then the amount transferred attracts tax at either the full rate (on death within three years) or at a reduced rate over the balance of the period. Similarly, a transfer of assets into an accumulation and maintenance trust, a disabled person's trust or a trust in which an individual has an interest in possession are all potentially exempt transfers. Transfers or gifts to other forms of trusts attract

48

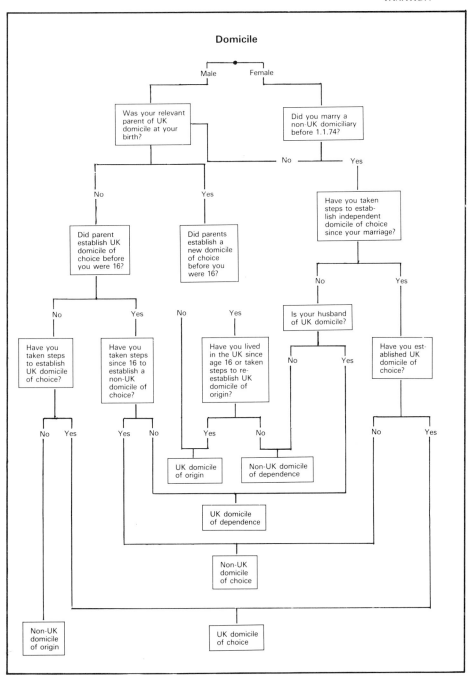

Domicile

inheritance tax at 50 per cent of the full rate (see Appendix I). A further form of transfer highlighted by the new IHT rules is a "gift with reservation". If, for example, someone decided to make a gift of certain assets but retained the right to enjoy them — a common example would be the family home — then such a gift would be a gift with reservation. Where such gifts are made the transfer is only deemed to have occurred at the time the reservation is removed. If, therefore, you continue to live in the family home until your death then the reservation would not be removed until that time, and the transfer being made then would attract tax at the full rate.

The various reliefs and exemptions which applied to capital transfer tax are continued for inheritance tax, the main ones being as follows:

Annual allowance
Each year a person may transfer £3,000 free from any liability or potential liability to IHT. This may be carried forward for one year if unused but only to the extent that the current year's allowance has been utilised. For example, a person makes no gifts in 1986/87, then gives away £5,000 in 1987/88. The exemption given will be £3,000 for 1987/88 and £2,000 for 1986/87. The remaining £1,000 of exemption for 1986/87 will be lost if it is not used before 6th April 1988.

Small gifts allowance
Up to £250 may be given to as many donees as the donor wishes in any one year.

Transfers between spouses
Where both spouses are UK domiciled such transfers are tax exempt. Where there is a transfer to a non-domiciled spouse the exemption limit is £55,000.

Gifts to charities and certain national institutions
There is unlimited scope for exempt gifts to these bodies.

Gifts out of income
Taking one year with another, if gifts can be shown to have been made out of income then there is no liability to IHT. But the donor should beware of giving away substantial income to others and then claiming to live off capital. Such a claim will not be accepted.

Other gifts
Special exemptions are also given for gifts in consideration at marriage, ie wedding presents, both between intending spouses and from relatives.

Also retained from the CTT regime is the valuation of a transfer. This remains the amount of loss to the donor rather than the value to the donee.

On the face of it there is no need to plan for IHT. Simply give everything away and survive for seven years and no tax need be paid. However, this is hardly realistic. The previously CTT-effective inheritance trusts, PETA plans and discounted gift schemes were among the first casualties of the new rules. The gifts with reservation and the non-allowance of certain estate debts under IHT completely rule these out. For most expatriates the simplest form of IHT planning, after making a will, will be to take a long term approach to providing for the ultimate liability while, at the same time, making use of such exemptions and potentially exempt transfers as they can afford. Ultimate provision may usefully be made through whole of life assurance policies written in trust for the beneficiaries. Also, where a large potentially exempt transfer is made, it may be worthwhile taking out a decreasing term assurance policy to cover potential tax during the subsequent seven years. Similarly, investment-oriented insurance policies can be written in trust and where large lump sums are available but some continuing income is required, a gift and loan scheme is possible. Under such a scheme the donor receives a return of his loan to say 5 per cent a year while the underlying investment growth accrues to his heirs.

Although the rates have been simplified and the rate bands extended, IHT remains a highly progressive tax and for wealthy expatriates can have a major impact on what they leave to their children. Attitudes to such effects vary from individual to individual. There are those who take the view that whatever their children receive they should be grateful for, and if the taxman has taken a large slice before they get it, that is of little consequence. On the other hand, there are those who are determined to prevent the Inland Revenue getting anything at all. The compromise approach which most people adopt can only be found by a full discussion with a financial advisor which takes account of all family circumstances and resources available.

UK TAXES — VALUE ADDED TAX

British value added tax is rarely a problem for the expatriate and it requires but a brief mention in this book. On the positive side the expatriate or intending expatriate may be able to buy many items, from clothing to motor cars, in the UK without having to pay the VAT normally charged. The position regarding cars for export was discussed in chapter 2 (p20). Other items which the expatriate requires VAT-free have to be bought from suppliers who advertise, or who are prepared to give, an export service. There can be a lot of paper work involved and the goods must be shipped overseas directly. For the expatriate who intends buying a whole new wardrobe or several expensive luxury items such an exercise is probably worthwhile, but rarely otherwise.

There are, however, occasions when the expatriate will have to pay VAT. These most commonly arise in connection with UK property. Legal fees for services concerned with land or property and leases of property do attract VAT. So, too, do the costs of repairs and maintenance work on UK properties. Services related to property such as architects' and surveyors' costs are also chargeable. Property service charges may or may not be subject to VAT depending on how the charge is operated.

Finally, on the supply of services generally, whether or not the service is VAT-able will also be affected by the country in which the supplier belongs. If, for example, an expatriate seeks advice from his UK-based accountant then the subsequent bill will rightly include a charge for VAT. If, on the other hand, the expatriate received his advice from the Jersey office of his accountant's practice, no VAT would be chargeable. In most cases, unless the services are to be used in the UK, VAT will be at the zero rate. However, if the customer or client is resident within the EEC and the service is provided to him in his personal capacity, the normal rate may be payable.

OVERSEAS TAXES — DOUBLE TAXATION AGREEMENTS

The British resident can generally avoid double taxation of his overseas income either by unilateral relief granted by the Inland Revenue or through the specific provisions of a double taxation agreement. Agreements generally allow for some form of credit to be given in the country of residence for tax paid in the country where the income arises, or alternatively, might exempt income where it arises on the basis that it will be taxed in the recipient's country of residence. Agreements do vary, however, and the definition of residence is not always the same as the UK definition. Indeed, where there is a double taxation agreement this will normally provide for an individual's residence position to be established under the terms of the agreement which will over-ride the normal provisions contained in the two parties' domestic legislation.

The UK is party to a large network of double taxation agreements and countries operating those relating to taxes on income and capital gains are listed below. Copies of current agreements can be obtained from the Inland Revenue.

Antigua	Gambia	Luxembourg	Sierra Leone
Australia	Germany	Malawi	Singapore
Austria	Ghana	Malaysia	Solomon Is
Bangladesh	Greece	Malta	South Africa
Barbados	Grenada	Mauritius	Spain
Belgium	Guernsey	Montserrat	Sri Lanka
Belize	Hungary	Namibia	Sudan
Botswana	India	Netherlands	Swaziland
Brunei	Indonesia	N'lands Ant's	Sweden
Burma	Ireland	New Zealand	Switzerland
Canada	Isle of Man	Nigeria	Thailand
China	Israel	Norway	Trinidad and
Cyprus	Italy	Pakistan	Tobago
Denmark	Ivory Coast	Philippines	Tunisia
Dominica	Jamaica	Poland	Turkey
Egypt	Japan	Portugal	Tuvalu
Falkland Is	Jersey	Romania	Uganda
Faroe Is	Kenya	St Kitts-Nevis	USA
Fiji	Kiribati	St Lucia	USSR
Finland	Korea	St Vincent	Yugoslavia
France	Lesotho	Seychelles	Zambia
			Zimbabwe

Most modern double taxation agreements follow the OECD model, parts of which are reproduced in Appendix II.

In addition to the double taxation agreements on income and capital gains taxes there are others which relate to capital taxes.

Expatriates living and working in the countries listed above will be able to obtain a measure of relief from certain UK tax they might otherwise have been liable to pay, but of perhaps more interest will be taxation on income arising in a third country. To find out about other agreements it will be necessary to approach the taxation authorities in the country concerned. Double taxation agreements are complex and generally written in technical language, and professional advice should be taken before relying on a personal interpretation of the provisions.

4

National Insurance

CONTRIBUTIONS PAYABLE BY EXPATRIATES

The previous chapter illustrated the complexity of the UK tax legislation and how the expatriate may, in certain circumstances, have a continuing UK tax liability. The legislation relating to social security and National Insurance is no less complicated and, as with tax, the expatriate may have a continuing liability to pay National Insurance contributions too. Apart from any mandatory payment of National Insurance, the non-resident will also have the option of making a voluntary payment in order to keep his contribution record up to date so as to safeguard his entitlement to pensions and other benefits.

National Insurance payments

National Insurance payments in the UK fall into one of four classes:

Class 1 contributions are paid by employees earning more than a minimum amount (for 1987/88 that limit is fixed at £39.00 per week). The amount payable is directly related to earnings between the lower limit and a maximum (£295 per week in 1987/88). Class 1 contributions count for all benefits.

Class 2 contributions are payable by the self-employed at a flat rate of £3.85 per week in 1987/88. These contributions count only for the basic rate of retirement and widows' pensions, sickness and invalidity benefit and a few other minor benefits.

Class 3 contributions are voluntary payments which can be made to protect the individual's rights to basic pensions where he is not contributing under any other class of payment. The 1987/88 rate is £3.75 per week.

Class 4 contributions are also payable by the self-employed with earnings between set limits (£4,590 to £15,340 in 1987/88). These contributions are a straight levy of 6.3 per cent and count for no benefits whatsoever.

Expatriate National Insurance contributions may be any of the first three classes depending on individual circumstances and preference, whether or not the employer has a UK base or is an international government agency, or on the expatriate's country of residence.

Class 1 contributions abroad

An expatriate must pay Class 1 contributions for his first 52 weeks abroad in the following circumstances:

(1) he is under retirement age; and
(2) his employer has a place of business in the UK; and
(3) he is 'ordinarily resident' in the UK; and
(4) he was resident in the UK immediately before taking up the overseas employment.

Contributions will be at the same rate as if the expatriate had been living in the UK. The Department of Health and Social Security does not define the term 'ordinarily resident' and neither does it have the same meaning as it has in taxation terms although there are certain similarities. But as a rule of thumb, a person will continue to be treated as ordinarily resident for DHSS purposes if he intends to return to the UK within three years of departure. Where the overseas stay is longer than three years, the DHSS will decide on residence status in the light of the individual facts and will take into account the expected duration of overseas service, whether or not a home is being retained in the UK, and what has been done with furniture and personal effects. The tendency is to consider an expatriate as ordinarily resident unless he goes abroad indefinitely, sells up his UK property and disposes of his belongings.

Class 1 contributions may be paid voluntarily if the expatriate works for certain employers such as foreign governments or agencies such as the UN, WHO, the EEC Commission and the like. Payment may be made for the first 52 weeks only.

Voluntary contributions abroad

Class 1 contributions can only be paid voluntarily for 52 weeks and only in the restricted circumstances mentioned above. Thereafter any voluntary contributions have to be made by Class 2 or Class 3 payment. Class 2 payments may be made in the following instances:

(1) either the expatriate has lived in the UK for a continuous three-year period at any time; or
(2) before going abroad he paid a set minimum amount of contributions for three years or more; and
(3) he is working abroad; and
(4) he was employed or self-employed immediately before going abroad.

To pay voluntary Class 3 contributions only the first condition or the second condition relating to Class 2 need be fulfilled. If either Class 2 or Class 3 contributions are paid the expatriate can change from one to the other at any time except that he cannot change from Class 3 to Class 2 if he is not employed. Class 2 contributions are marginally more expensive than Class 3 (10p per week at the present time) but they qualify the payer for sickness and invalidity benefit on return to the UK. However, expatriates who have paid Class 1 contributions for their first 52 weeks abroad need not choose to pay Class 2 for that reason, since they will be treated as if they had paid during their whole time abroad so long as they remained ordinarily resident. In the same way the Class 1 payer may also be entitled to unemployment benefit or maternity allowance, neither of which are provided by any amount of Class 2 or Class 3 payments.

Reciprocal agreements and employment within the EEC
Special rules apply to expatriates working in countries with whom the UK has a reciprocal agreement and in member countries of the EEC. Countries with reciprocal agreements are listed at Note 1 on the flow chart on page 57. These agreements vary from country to country but they generally allow for expatriates working there for more than twelve months to join the local social security scheme and to be given credit in the UK on return for any contributions made there. In addition, UK contributions may be counted in the other country towards any benefit which may be payable there. Detailed advice on these arrangements and those for EEC countries can be obtained from the Overseas Branch of the DHSS.

Payment of voluntary contributions
Application to pay voluntary Class 2 or Class 3 contributions should be made on form CF83 which is included in the DHSS leaflet NI138. Payment can be made either by direct debit of a UK bank account, by an annual payment direct to the DHSS Overseas Branch, or by a paying agent in the UK. Payment should be made at the end of each tax year and in any event must be paid before the end of the sixth tax year following the year to which they relate; that is arrears of up to six years can be accepted. For example, contributions due for the tax year 1987/88 must be paid by 5th April 1994.

Are voluntary payments worthwhile?
As a general rule the answer is yes. By maintaining a full National Insurance record the expatriate will protect his right to a full retirement or widow's pension. For an index-linked investment the low 'premium' rate of a few pounds each week represents very good value. Full entitlement to retirement and widow's pension does not, in fact, require a 100 per cent contribution record. Contributions must, however, be paid over 9/10ths of the claimant's working life. In practical terms this means that a man may miss a maximum of four-and-a-half years contributions before his pension rights are curtailed. It must, however, be noted that where someone attended university for say three or four years and did not pay National Insurance during that period then that leeway is effectively exhausted. For those, on the other hand, who started work immediately on leaving school they could on a relatively short overseas contract miss out on National Insurance contributions without suffering at the end of the day.

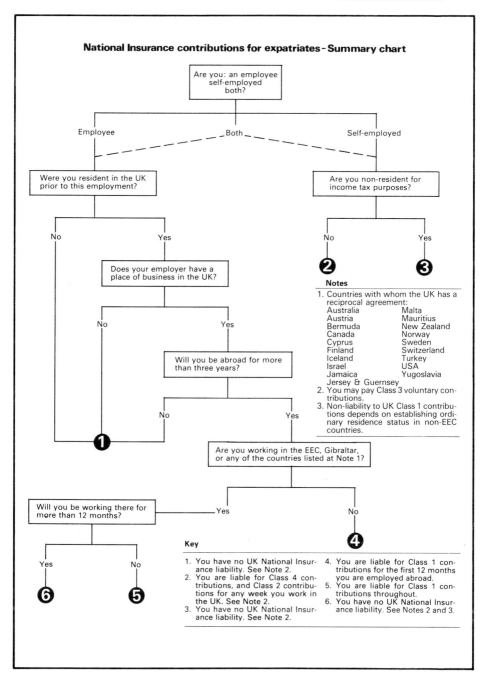

National Insurance contributions for expatriates - Summary chart

Are you: an employee
self-employed
both?

Employee — Both — Self-employed

Were you resident in the UK prior to this employment?

Are you non-resident for income tax purposes?

No — Yes

No — Yes

❷   ❸

Notes
1. Countries with whom the UK has a reciprocal agreement:

Australia	Malta
Austria	Mauritius
Bermuda	New Zealand
Canada	Norway
Cyprus	Sweden
Finland	Switzerland
Iceland	Turkey
Israel	USA
Jamaica	Yugoslavia
Jersey & Guernsey	

2. You may pay Class 3 voluntary contributions.
3. Non-liability to UK Class 1 contributions depends on establishing ordinary residence status in non-EEC countries.

Does your employer have a place of business in the UK?

No — Yes

Will you be abroad for more than three years?

No — Yes

❶

Are you working in the EEC, Gibraltar, or any of the countries listed at Note 1?

Will you be working there for more than 12 months? — Yes — No

❹

Yes — No

❻   ❺

Key
1. You have no UK National Insurance liability. See Note 2.
2. You are liable for Class 4 contributions, and Class 2 contributions for any week you work in the UK. See Note 2.
3. You have no UK National Insurance liability. See Note 2.
4. You are liable for Class 1 contributions for the first 12 months you are employed abroad.
5. You are liable for Class 1 contributions throughout.
6. You have no UK National Insurance liability. See Notes 2 and 3.

BENEFITS PAYABLE TO EXPATRIATES

Britain operates one of the most comprehensive social welfare pro-grammes in the world, but it is intended for those people living in this country, not for those who choose to go overseas. However, there are certain benefits which can be paid abroad or which can be enjoyed by non-residents. Mention has already been made in the first part of this chapter of reciprocal agreements and special arrangements within the EEC and how these may operate to give the expatriate a claim to local benefits. Individual details should be obtained from the DHSS Overseas Branch.

Pensions and the National Health Service

The benefits of greatest interest to expatriates are pensions — retire-ment and widows' — and medical services under the National Health Service. Pensions can be paid anywhere in the world and the only variation is in the amount actually payable. In general, the pension will be paid at either the rate in force when the person retires or is widowed, if living abroad at the time, or the rate in force at the time the person goes overseas. Annual pension increases are not normally payable to someone living abroad. Where the non-resident returns to the UK on a visit the current rate will be paid but payment will revert to the lower level once more on departure.

But as with all general rules, there are exceptions. Expatriates who live in certain countries with reciprocal agreements do have their pension increases allowed, as do those living in the EEC. Not all countries with reciprocal agreements, however, deal with pensions in the same way. The agreements with Australia and Canada do not cover pensions at all, and the agreements with Bermuda, Portugal, Jamaica and the USA apply only to increases which accrued after the agreement came into force, so the actual pension level for older expatriates will be lower than in the UK.

So far as health services are concerned, there are also reciprocal health agreements but these apply in the main to short term visitors. Most expatriates will need to be either privately insured or a contri-butor to the local health scheme or both to be sure of adequate treatment abroad. Treatment in the UK will still be possible for most expatriates despite recent changes in the legislation applying to UK visitors. A person who has lived continuously in the UK for ten years and then goes abroad to work will still be entitled to free treatment on the NHS during visits to the UK so long as he has not been abroad for more than five years. Where his overseas service is greater than five years he may still be entitled to free treatment if he visits the UK regularly or if his employer is under a contractual obligation to provide the expatriate with one passage home each year (whether or not he actually comes home). A return to the UK specifically for medical treatment is allowed but the expatriate should beware of the lengthy waiting lists at most NHS hospitals.

Other benefits

Other benefits can be paid to expatriates in certain circumstances. These are explained briefly below.

Child benefit

Where someone is going abroad, with or without a child for whom benefit is payable for a period not expected to exceed eight weeks, then benefit can continue. Where the overseas period continues beyond eight weeks or if it is expected so to do from the start, benefit ceases from the date of departure. Where the child remains in the UK and a UK resident has care and control of that child, ie a guardian, relative, etc, then that relative or guardian can claim child benefit for that child or children. This can be particularly useful when children are at school in the UK and a relative is appointed to look after their interests. The benefit can continue without time limit so long as the situation remains.

Child's special allowance and guardian's allowance

These allowances may be paid anywhere abroad if the beneficiary's absence, and that of the child, is only temporary. Annual increases are paid only in the EEC and countries with reciprocal agreements.

Widowed mother's allowance

This benefit, including increases for children, may be paid anywhere abroad if the absence from the UK is only temporary. A widowed mother living abroad permanently can get the personal element of the allowance if the child is living with her. She cannot get any increase of benefit for the child.

Maternity grant

This may be paid overseas provided that the normal National Insurance contributions applicable are met.

Sickness benefit, invalidity benefit, and maternity allowance

These can be paid abroad if the conditions of the EEC social security regulations or of a reciprocal agreement are met. These may also cover increases paid each year.

Unemployment benefit

This can be paid outside the UK but only in another EEC country. To get this the person claiming must be registered as unemployed in Britain for at least four weeks before wishing to go abroad. He is then allowed to look for work in another EEC country for up to three months and UK unemployment benefit can continue for this time.

Attendance allowance and mobility allowance

Anyone who has been receiving either or both of these benefits can continue to receive them during a temporary absence abroad for up to six months. Either benefit can be paid for a longer period abroad if this is for the specific purpose of getting treatment for an illness or disablement which began before leaving the UK.

Invalid care allowance

This can also be paid during a temporary absence abroad.

Death grant
This can be paid for a person who dies abroad. However, not only must the deceased have met the usual National Insurance contributions, he (or she) must also have met, immediately prior to death, any one of a number of special conditions. These include entitlement to a retirement pension, widow's benefit or industrial death benefit, sickness, industrial injuries or, for a woman dying in childbirth, maternity benefit. Death grant may also be paid if the deceased was employed as a mariner, a member of the cabin crew of a civil aircraft, a member of HM forces, or worked on the UK continental shelf area at the time of death. People ordinarily resident in the UK who die within 13 weeks of leaving the country may also qualify.

Industrial injury benefits
Benefits for accidents or diseases arising from employment overseas cannot generally be paid by the UK unless under the terms of the EEC regulations or a reciprocal agreement. Where benefit is already in payment on leaving the UK, the following applies:

(1) *Injury benefit:* unless the EEC regulations or reciprocal agreement conditions are met, injury benefit can only be paid abroad for temporary absences for the specific purpose of receiving treatment for the injury.
(2) *Disablement pensions, gratuities and industrial death benefit:* these can be paid anywhere abroad at the full current UK rate.

Constant attendance allowance
This can usually be paid during the first three months of temporary absence from the UK as long as the absence is not for the purpose of work.

War pensions
Anyone who is a war pensioner can generally get his war disablement pension or allowance paid anywhere in the world at the same rates as those current in the UK.

Benefits available from each class of National Insurance contribution

Class 1	Class 2	Class 3
Unemployment	Sickness (basic)	Maternity grant
Sickness	Invalidity (basic)	Widow's pension
Invalidity	Maternity	Retirement pension
Industrial injuries	Widow's pension	Child's special
Disablement & death	Retirement pension	allowance
Maternity	Guardian's	Death grant
Widow's pension	allowance	
Retirement pension	Child's special	
Guardian's	allowance	
allowance	Death grant	
Child's special		
allowance		
Death grant		

5

Investment and financial planning

For many readers this chapter may be the one that they are most interested in, it may even be why they bought the book in the first place. Money remains one of the major reasons why people go to work abroad but for many of them financial planning is akin to the black arts. Never having had more than a couple of small life policies, a few pounds in the building society and perhaps some premium bonds, the idea of handling hundreds, thousands, or even tens of thousands of pounds of savings is for some expatriates a daunting if attractive prospect. It is not made any easier by the often strident and competing claims of the many investments promoted to expatriates, not to mention the array of financial services offered by a multitude of advisors.

My aim with this chapter is, so far as possible, to consider the entire spectrum of family finances in a logical and realistic way, taking in the basics of financial protection, proper banking requirements, pensions and investments. Many readers will already know much of what follows, but for them it might be a useful "refresher course" on what financial planning is all about, or a checklist to ensure nothing vital has been missed.

By way of setting the scene the following is a synopsis of how Mr and Mrs New Expatriate (and later Mr and Mrs Experienced Expatriate) should go about putting their finances in order.

Overseas job offer arrives
(1) Buy Working Abroad — The Expatriate's Guide.
(2) Subscribe to one or more of the main expatriate publications (see chapter 10).
(3) Review existing investments, insurances, and banking arrangements.
(4) Check overseas salary payment arrangements, discuss with your own bank your additional requirements and check which is their correspondent bank in your overseas location. Arrange opening of offshore savings account.
(5) Review your protection requirements — life assurance, medical cover, personal effects, etc.

Arrival overseas and first three to six months
(6) Money disappears like magic.
(7) Eventually the overdraft is repaid.

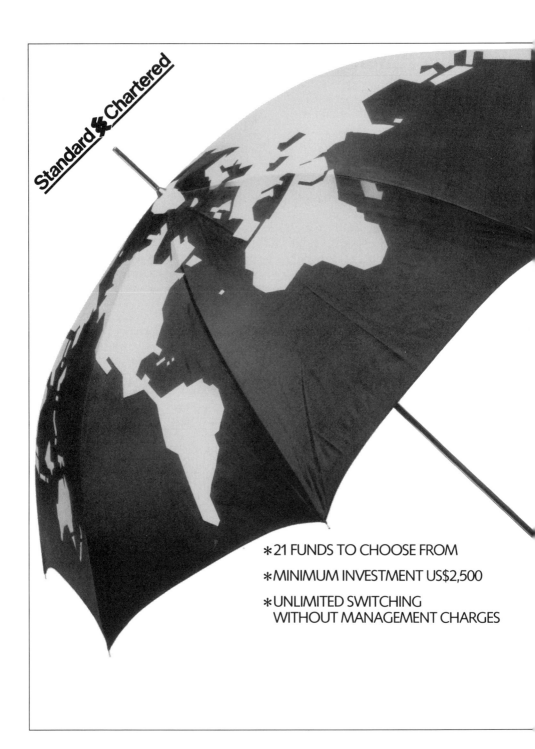

*21 FUNDS TO CHOOSE FROM

*MINIMUM INVESTMENT US$2,500

*UNLIMITED SWITCHING
 WITHOUT MANAGEMENT CHARGES

Next six to nine months
(8) Spending pattern becomes more settled and hopefully expenditure is less than income.
(9) Income surplus is held on deposit or in a high interest cheque account.
(10) Consider what provision, if any, needs to be given to long term income provision — ie pension planning.

Year two
(11) Regular savings can now be quantified and some decisions made on savings priorities.
(12) A cash reserve has been built up in an offshore savings account.
(13) Consult a professional financial advisor of good repute, preferably one who comes via trusted personal recommendation, for an investment strategy.
(14) Be advised, if appropriate, on a suitable flexible pension plan, school fee plan, or provision for any other definite medium/long term requirement. These provisions should **not** require the whole of your regular savings.
(15) Be advised on a short/medium term immediate access investment portfolio.

Years three, four, . . .
(16) Continue to build up your assets.
(17) Have regular consultations with your advisor, keeping him informed of any changes in circumstances, both windfalls and new liabilities.

Year ? — homecoming
(18) Inform your advisor as soon as you can that you will be returning to the UK.
(19) Your advisor will review all accounts, investments, pensions and insurances for tax effectiveness in the UK and recommend any necessary changes.
(20) Close your local current account and spend your remaining riyals on a coke at the airport bar.

Home at last to a carefree, financially secure future.

If only things were that easy or went so smoothly. Hidden among these 20 points are innumerable pitfalls and traps for the unwary. Most of these can be avoided, some result simply from bad luck. The remainder of this chapter should save you from the former, but keeping rubbing the rabbit's foot.

UK INVESTMENTS
Many expatriates will already hold certain investments when they go abroad and it is likely that these will be UK based. As elements in an overall investment strategy these may be perfectly acceptable but they must be reviewed to ensure their appropriateness for non-residents.

Bank and building society deposits

As mentioned in chapter 3, where the deposits are owned by UK residents the interest on these accounts is paid net of tax but where the depositor is not ordinarily resident for UK tax purposes then interest may be paid gross. This situation is quite satisfactory while the expatriate is abroad but during his year of return to the UK the whole of any interest paid during that year is taxable. For this reason it is better for the expatriate to hold any cash deposits outside the UK in order that all interest up to his time of return can be made tax free.

Life assurance policies

Investment-oriented life assurance is probably the most popular investment medium after building societies for UK residents. For regular premium policies prior to 1984 there was the incentive of tax relief on the premiums paid, "tax free" proceeds at maturity and, in the case of single premium policies, tax free withdrawals and other advantages. Life assurance premium relief was withdrawn on new policies from March 1984 but in other respects the regime remains as it was, but for an expatriate going to perhaps a tax free environment the "tax free" proceeds of UK policies should be considered quite closely. While the proceeds may attract no further tax in the hands of the policyholder, they will have been subject to tax in the hands of the insurance company. Income tax on the income of the underlying investments and any capital gains are charged directly to the insurance company. However, where regular premium policies are concerned it is rarely advisable to dispense with these on going abroad as the penalties for early surrender can be substantial. It is important, however, not to take out any additional investment-oriented insurance in the UK before becoming an expatriate. Single premium policies might usefully be disposed of but much will depend on the expatriate's particular tax situation and each case needs to be examined on its own merits. Obviously, where an endowment policy is being used as collateral for a mortgage then this must be continued.

National savings

These are attractive to UK residents, largely for tax reasons. Their appeal is largely lost when the holder goes abroad. National Savings Income Bonds pay gross, as does the National Savings Bank, but both suffer in the same way as other bank and building society deposits in the year of return. The fact that they offer attractive interest rates should be weighed against this latter disadvantage. Premium bonds are held by many expatriates and certainly those who hold one or two thousand pounds worth seem to reap a regular, if relatively small, return. However, the chance of becoming one of the large prize-winners gives these bonds their basic attraction and for a portfolio of any size some small exposure to this form of gambling need not be too strongly discouraged.

UK government stock

UK Government debt or gilts has been a traditional mainstay of British expatriate investment for many years. On occasion they can produce very reasonable returns in terms of both interest and capital growth and many stocks permit gross payment of interest to those who are not ordinarily resident in the UK. The exempt stocks, ie those which permit gross payment, are listed below:

9%	Conversion Stock 2000	9½%	Treasury Loan 1999
11%	Exchequer Loan 1990	10%	Treasury Loan 1991
13¼%	Exchequer Loan 1996	10%	Treasury Loan 1992
5¾%	Funding Loan 1987/91	10%	Treasury Loan 1993
6%	Funding Loan 1993	10%	Treasury Loan 1994
6¾%	Treasury Loan 1995/98	12½%	Treasury Loan 1993
7¾%	Treasury Loan 1985/88	12¾%	Treasury Loan 1992
7¾%	Treasury Loan 2012/15	12¾%	Treasury Loan 1995
8%	Treasury Loan 2002/06	13¼%	Treasury Loan 1997
8¼%	Treasury Loan 1987/90	13¾%	Treasury Loan 1993
8¾%	Treasury Loan 1997	14½%	Treasury Loan 1994
8½%	Treasury Loan 2000	15¼%	Treasury Loan 1996
9%	Treasury Loan 1992/96	15½%	Treasury Loan 1998
9%	Treasury Loan 1994	5½%	Treasury Stock 2008/12
8½%	Treasury Loan 2007	13%	Treasury Stock 1990
9%	Treasury Loan 2008	3½%	War Loan 1952 or after

Unit trusts
Investment in UK unit trusts is perfectly acceptable by non-residents except where the trusts concerned produce a high income yield. In these cases the dividend distributed is effectively net of tax which in most cases is not reclaimable by the expatriate (subject to a Section 27 claim and/or a double taxation agreement — see chapter 3). Growth-oriented unit trusts incur little or no tax liability on the part of the non-resident holder. These are touched upon further in this chapter.

Equities
Shares in UK companies can be considered in much the same light as unit trusts — leaving aside their obviously higher risk except where the portfolio is extensive — and where they are held primarily for capital growth there is no objection to their use by expatriates.

Property
See later in this chapter (and also chapter 5).

EXPATRIATE BANKING SERVICES

Where to bank
The expatriate has certain basic banking requirements. These are that his funds should be secure, easily accessible, and freely transferrable. He will require a current or chequing account for any continuing commitment in the UK and another for day-to-day expenses in local currency overseas. He should also have a deposit or interest-bearing account in which to accumulate a cash reserve, and he may possibly

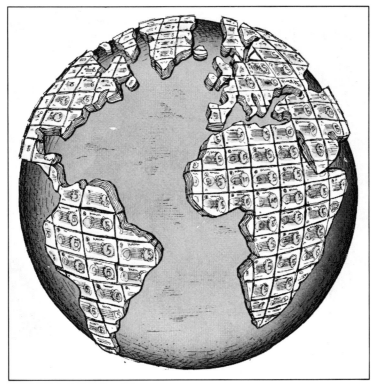

GT MANAGES OVER $6 BILLION* WORTH OF INVESTMENTS AROUND THE WORLD.
_(*at 31.3.87.)

The amount of money we manage around the globe is quite remarkable.

It has been entrusted to us by thousands of investors because of our considerable success in making money for them over the years.

We believe we have achieved this success because of our commitment to building an international investment network.

There are GT offices not only in the UK, but around Europe, the Far East, Australia and the USA.

Our expertise is available to you through a number of different funds.

To find out which one is best for you, send off for our free brochure now, or ask your financial adviser.

GT A WORLD OF INVESTMENT OPPORTUNITIES

require some of the more specialist banking services. Many expatriates do nothing about banking when they go abroad. They retain their existing account with one of the UK clearing banks, rely on their local manager, and either transfer regular sums abroad (if they are paid in the UK) or remit sums home (if they are paid overseas). This is by no means an efficient arrangement. A much better alternative is described below.

For an expatriate to make the best use of his bank, his bank must be fully aware of the problems and requirements of expatriates. The average UK high street bank manager is not in this position. Although most of the clearing banks now have some form of expatriate advisory service, many customers are still not referred to the specialist. Most expatriate experience and expertise in British banking is to be found in the offshore branches of the UK clearing banks in the Channel Islands or Isle of Man and it is to these branches that the expatriate should look for his banking requirements. All the usual facilities available on the mainland are equally available in the Channel Islands and Isle of Man branches. These include cheque guarantee and credit cards, automatic cash dispenser facilities, statements as and when required, and, perhaps most important of all, the same interest rates as applicable in the UK mainland — but invariably paid gross.

The expatriate or intending expatriate need not, therefore, change his bank; instead he need only change his branch from the UK mainland to offshore. Some banks recommend that an existing current account is left undisturbed and only a deposit account opened offshore. This is acceptable but it might appear preferable to have the complete banking service contained under one roof. If at all possible, the expatriate should aim to have his salary credited directly to an interest-bearing account (less, if the option is available, a sum to cover local living expenses). Some banks allow free transfers from a deposit account each month for the purpose of feeding a current account from which may be paid all standing orders, direct debits, other regular payments not normally allowed from deposit accounts. The advent of high interest cheque accounts in recent years has made this type of arrangement somewhat easier.

Where the expatriate's salary is paid to a bank in the country in which he works he should try to ensure that the bank used is a correspondent bank of his home bank. In that way the transfer of funds to his bank in Jersey or wherever can be made more rapidly and perhaps more cheaply. Similarly, if funds have to be transferred to the expatriate this can be most conveniently done by a transfer to a correspondent bank. Most UK banks can also offer current accounts in major foreign currencies but these are generally less acceptable than local bank current accounts — certainly if you are paying for goods by cheque overseas.

Savings accounts

Moving on from current accounts to savings accounts, these should represent the first part of an expatriate's (or indeed anyone else's) investment strategy. A liquid cash reserve should be the first priority. How large this reserve should be will obviously depend on individual circumstances and intentions, but somewhere between £2,000 and £10,000 should be sufficient. Most other investments should be treated as medium to long term commitments and a sudden requirement for cash could involve the investor in a loss which might be avoided if the investment were undisturbed for a further period. It is primarily for that reason that a fair cash reserve is necessary. But it must also be productive. The least productive but most liquid deposit account from the clearing banks has been the 7-day deposit, where withdrawals can be made either with 7 days notice or immediately with the loss of 7 days interest. However, as mentioned above, most clearing banks now operate accounts which offer interest. These high interest cheque accounts have certain restrictions, commonly in a minimum balance of £2,000 or £2,500 and a minimum withdrawal of £200 or more plus fairly significant charges. That said, they still represent the most liquid way of holding a cash reserve with the convenience of withdrawals by cheque, direct debit, telegraphic transfer, etc. Interest rates tend to be very good on these accounts at least in terms of immediately available rates. Less liquid forms of cash deposits may offer slightly higher rates, the penalty being 90 days or 6 months notice. Term accounts such as these cannot really be described as liquid reserve accounts although most banks will be prepared to advance a loan against the maturity of such term deposits but you may rest assured that the interest charged will be higher than the interest you will receive.

There is also a problem with term deposits when the expatriate is due to return to the UK. Closing an offshore bank account can prevent the interest up to the date of closure being taxed in the UK but attempting to close a term deposit before the maturity date will either incur a significant interest penalty or will simply not be allowable.

Joint accounts
Joint accounts can be problematical. Unless both spouses are non-resident for tax purposes these should be avoided, otherwise there will be a tax liability either because a non-working spouse may be unable to sign the not ordinarily resident declaration for UK banks or the gross interest paid offshore can be taxable in the wife's name.

Foreign currency deposit accounts
Like foreign currency current accounts, foreign currency deposit accounts are available from the British banks. Accounts in all the world's major currencies are freely available and other currency accounts can be opened if the sums involved are large enough. For most expatriates, however, these accounts are unlikely to be of much benefit. If the expatriate sees himself as a currency speculator he would be wise to forget it as soon as possible. Currencies are highly volatile and the delay of even a few hours can make the difference between a gain and a loss. Few individuals have the facilities for keeping close enough to the market and instructing their bank in the timescales involved. A foreign currency account might be useful as a hedge but it should not account for more than five per cent to ten per cent of the individual's total assets. In any case there are profession-

ally managed currency funds which are much more appropriate for the private investor. The only other occasion when a foreign currency account may be appropriate is where the expatriate is paid in, say, US dollars, he spends his holidays in the USA and intends to move there permanently. For other British expatriates sterling should be the main cash reserved currency.

Foreign banks
So far, this section has dealt primarily with what the UK banks and their offshore branches have to offer. There are, of course, many other banks which will welcome the expatriate's business with open arms and provide him with an excellent service. In the UK, although there is competition among the banks the interest rates tend to be very similar from one bank to another. This is not always the case else-where and substantial differences can sometimes be found. But the old investment truism — the greater the reward, the higher the risk — should never be forgotten. Banks offering interest rates significantly out of line with the general run should be immediately suspect.

Another aspect of banking which may concern some expatriates is secrecy or the lack of it, in particular the passing of information to Revenue authorities. Traditionally, the Swiss banks are the ultimate in secrecy and discretion although the banking services of all tax havens claim similar immunity from external interference. These days it would be naive to suggest that any bank is 100 per cent safe from information leaks. In part, this is caused by the ever-increasing use of computer systems which, despite their sophistication and built in security measures have succumbed to the efforts of determined "hackers". Some international banks can be susceptible to pressure from the authorities in their head office location for information held by overseas branches or subsidiaries. These, however, are still infrequent problems and it must be asked whether or not such leaks are important to most British expatriates. Generally speaking the answer is no unless the intent is tax evasion. Of much greater impor-tance is the financial probity of the bank. One way of being reasonably sure of this is to deal only with major banking institutions in countries with stringent banking rules and checks.

To summarise, most expatriates require three bank accounts — a UK current account for ongoing commitments, an offshore savings account to build up a cash reserve, and a local current account for expenditure in their country of residence.

INSURANCE AND PROTECTION

Existing policies
Life assurance as an investment medium has been mentioned earlier and forms no part of an expatriate's basic protective requirements. Where the expatriate already holds protective life cover — term assurance or whole of life policies, these can be continued when he goes abroad. It is, however, important to check with older policies that there are no restrictions imposed on the expatriate's residence and if

WOULDN'T YOU BE BETTER OFF WITH JUST ONE FINANCIAL ADVISER?

The trouble with having more than one investment company, is that your affairs are often handled by too many people.

Unfortunately, this can lead to all manner of confusion and problems. For example you could end up holding too many US Dollars or being over-exposed in Japan.

To help you avoid these problems, Hill Samuel can centralize the management of your affairs in one readily accessible location.

Which means you won't run the risk of imbalanced currency holdings or overexposure in any one market.

So why not call us or send off the coupon. Because talking to one person now, could mean dealing with far fewer later on.

To Michael Vlahovic, Hill Samuel Investment Services International S.A., 10 Rue Robert – Estienne, Geneva 1204, Switzerland. Tel. 201907.

Please tell me more about your services offered in Jersey ☐ Switzerland ☐.

I would like a personal adviser to call without obligation.

Name_____

Address_____

_____ Postcode_____

Home Tel._____ Business Tel._____

🏛 HILLSAMUEL
INVESTMENT SERVICES INTERNATIONAL

WA/11/87/EI

there are the policy will need to be either endorsed or replaced. Other protective policies such as accident and sickness, permanent health, family income benefit or medical insurance schemes are all likely to have overseas residence restrictions. In some cases it may be possible to have existing policies amended, invariably for an increased premium, but more usually a new policy will again be required. Property and personal effects insurance should also be checked. If a house is to be left vacant for a lengthy period then almost certainly the insurance policies both for building and contents will cease to apply, at least to the same level of cover. Insurers must be informed so that the proper cover at the appropriate premium (higher than before) can be issued.

For all types of insurance the services of a good broker are essential both for advice on existing arrangements or for new or replacement contracts. In many instances, of course, much of the personal cover the expatriate needs will be provided by his employer as part of his remuneration package. In such cases the expatriate need only ensure that the level of protection is sufficient, that where appropriate, other family members are included and, if there is a shortfall, provide personally for the balance. Of the many types of protective insurance available, those described below will be of greatest interest to the expatriate.

Family protection
Under this heading fall policies where benefits are paid on the death or disability of the breadwinner. Most obvious of these is straight-forward life assurance. For most expatriates this can best be effected through a term assurance policy. With this type of policy the benefit will be paid on the death of the person insured within a specified period — the term of the policy. These policies are generally inexpensive and simple to arrange. The sum assured and the term chosen will obviously vary with personal circumstances but a useful rule of thumb for basic cover might be to provide a capital sum of five to ten times the annual salary for a term long enough to encompass the period when any children will be undergoing their education. In the absence of any pension provision this amount will be insufficient and should be doubled. Term policies are available with a variety of options which give them a degree of flexibility. Common options include part payment of the sum assured in the event of severe permanent disability, provision for increasing the sum assured periodically, renewal of cover at the end of the term or convertability to other types of policy such as whole of life or endowment.

In addition to the capital sum assured under a life policy a continuing income for the family may also be necessary. This can be effected by a family income benefit policy, again issued for a set period with benefits continuing for a given number of years. Permanent health or disability benefit policies are expensive even in the UK and should, if at all possible, be negotiated as part of the salary package. If this is not feasible then local insurance companies abroad may be able to offer competitive rates with UK companies. It can be worth shopping around.

Medical insurance

Medical insurance is commonly provided for expatriates by their employers, but in the case of accompanied posts the employee should check that his family is also covered. Where insurance is not provided or is provided only for the employee he should look at the UK based insurers, provident associations, as well as any local schemes. Insurance cover for repatriation in the event of a serious illness should also be considered, especially in countries where the local medical services may be less than satisfactory.

Travel insurance and personal effects

For the expatriate who will be travelling extensively on the job there are many comprehensive travel insurance packages which will be suitable. These will cover the costs involved when items are lost in transit, additional expenses caused by flight delays or cancellation, medical bills and so on. Personal effects overseas may be insured locally although they can be covered by a UK policy. Items left in the UK are best insured in the UK. It is important to reiterate the necessity of informing the UK insurer that effects are left in an empty house, tenanted house, in store or whatever. Failure to notify the insurer may result in a refusal of any claim.

Miscellaneous risks

One risk run by most expatriates is that of being sent home at short notice. If this happens before the expatriate has achieved non-resident status for tax purposes, an early return to the UK can mean a large tax bill. Where the employee has been abroad for 365 days his salary and benefits may be exempt but he might still have a capital gains tax liability or liability on investment income. If the overseas work is cut short before the 365 day term the expatriate will be fully taxable on his overseas salary and benefits as well. Fortunately, this risk (known as tax contingency) can be insured against and can often be included in an expatriate insurance package.

For expatriate property owners a policy to cover legal expenses arising from tenancy disputes or the removal of squatters may also prove useful.

The value of a competent insurance broker has already been mentioned but what the intending expatriate should bear in mind is that these policies take time to arrange and should not therefore be left to the last minute before departure.

FINANCIAL ADVISORS AND INVESTMENT MANAGERS

Many expatriates run their own finances and investment portfolios highly successfully and derive great enjoyment from this. They may themselves be in the finance or investment business or, more commonly, investment has become a hobby in response to their newly acquired savings capacity. But they remain the minority. Most expatriates have neither the time, the experience, nor the interest in the arcane world of investment. Indeed many expatriates are somewhat frightened of it, which goes a long way to explaining why vast amounts of expatriate money lie languishing in high street banks and building societies.

Ideally, the expatriate should engage the services of a financial advisor as soon as he knows he is going to work abroad. While this book may provide much of the basic information and assistance the intending expatriate needs it cannot be a substitute for a personal discussion with an advisor who will be able to deal with all the individual circumstances attaching to particular families. If not immediately, then hopefully within a year or two of going abroad the expatriate will also need the services of an investment manager. This may be the same person as the first financial advisor or it may be a company specialising in investment management which does not provide other services such as taxation, insurance and so on. If the overall financial advice and the investment management are separate it is important that your advisor can liaise with the investment manager. However, for most expatriates these functions will be carried out by one and the same individual or company.

Finding the right advisor
Like most important decisions, selecting a financial advisor is difficult. At the end of the day the expatriate's reasoning will almost certainly be wholly subjective; he will choose the advisor who gives him the greatest confidence and with whom he feels easiest. But before getting to any decision there are certain questions to be asked and some guidelines which should prove helpful.

First and foremost the expatriate financial advisor must be qualified to give advice. By this I do not mean a membership of assorted learned bodies, a fistful of degrees or whatever, although these might not be entirely irrelevant. A proven track record, a sound reputation and if at all possible a trusted personal recommendation are the qualifications necessary. Following the introduction of the Financial Services Act investment advisors based in the UK must be licensed by the Savings and Investment Board either directly or through membership of one of the regulatory bodies. For personal financial services the appropriate body is FIMBRA (The Financial Intermediaries, Managers and Brokers Regulatory Association). Membership of FIMBRA does not necessarily provide any guarantee of the probity or expertise of the advisor but the Association does make fairly extensive enquiries and checks on potential members before accepting their application. In addition members are subject to spot checks and must provide regular information to the Association. The Association rules as to business practice and handling of client money are stringent and it is to be expected that the vast majority of members will obey these rules. Advisors based outside the UK do not have to comply with the Financial Services Act although investor protection legislation is becoming more common in many countries. It would be wrong to insist that every expatriate must only use an advisor who is a member of FIMBRA or any similar regulatory body as there are many highly competent advisors who are not and will not become members. Nonetheless, before choosing an unlicensed or unregulated advisor the expatriate should satisfy himself fully about that advisor's qualifications.

A good expatriate financial advisor will obviously have extensive

74

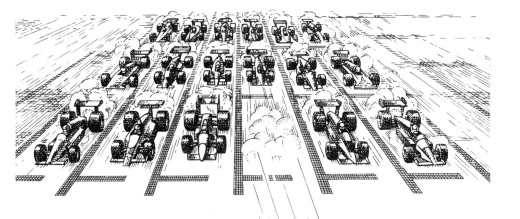

AT A DISTANCE, ALL PORTFOLIO MANAGEMENT SERVICES LOOK THE SAME

World investment opportunities are plentiful. They are also diverse, complex and fast moving. Professional management of your personal portfolio makes most sense – particularly when you live and work abroad.

But how do you distinguish, at arm's length, a service that offers real performance from one which could leave your funds on the starting grid?

Look closely.

Fidelity is the largest independent fund management group in the world. We manage private and institutional money exceeding $US 75 billion from our extensive research and investment facilities in London, Paris, Boston, Tokyo, Hong Kong, Jersey, Bermuda and Sydney – deploying local expertise to provide global perspective.

All of these resources are brought to bear in the International Portfolio Management Service, taking fullest account of your individual investment objectives. Close monitoring of offshore portfolios by our investment professionals provides an additional benefit – the reassurance that your investment will be constantly "tuned" to reflect prevailing market conditions.

Ask yourself how many other portfolio management services can even begin to provide this level of service for an initial investment of £20,000 ($30,000). Then decide who should receive the chequered flag.

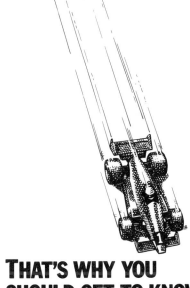

THAT'S WHY YOU SHOULD GET TO KNOW US

Fidelity
INTERNATIONAL

MAKING MONEY MAKE MONEY

knowledge of the particular problems which face expatriates — financial and non-financial — and will be technically competent in all aspects of UK tax as it applies to expatriates at all stages of their career — before, during, and after their period of expatriation. He will be familiar with insurance and pension requirements and those companies which provide the most suitable products for expatriates, and he will be wholly familiar with the entire spectrum of investments available to expatriates, in particular offshore funds, unit trusts and the like. If he is also an investment manager he will have a proper system for monitoring investments, dealing on an advisory or discretionary basis, and he should be able to demonstrate a satisfactory track record.

Financial advisors and investment managers come in all shapes and sizes from the one-man band to the major multi-national financial service companies. Most expatriates, however, draw their financial advice from one of the following categories:

Stockbrokers (mainly UK or US based)

Banks (clearing banks, merchant banks, occasionally Swiss or American banks)

Independent companies or firms (licensed dealers, trust companies, lawyers and accountants)

The expatriate magazines are generally full of advertisements from advisors in all of these categories and the expatriate potential client might usefully write to one or two managers in each category for details of the services they provide. The information provided should include details of charges, any in-house managed funds, links with other complimentary institutions including custodian and trustee arrangements, company accounts or financial statements and general background information. From this initial information the investor should select the most likely prospects and arrange a meeting. While some expatriates and some advisors are happy to deal entirely by post this cannot be considered a satisfactory arrangement. A personal meeting is essential from both the client and the advisor's point of view. At the meeting the client should meet both the senior manager and the person who will be in daily charge of his affairs. He should discuss all aspects of his requirements and, so far as investment management is concerned, the amount of discretion the manager has, to what extent he is required to follow company policy, what the manager's own background is, whether he deals on his own account and to what extent the company acts as both agent and principal. Although it is generally best for the investment manager to have complete discretion in the management of the investor's funds, there should be established from the start the parameters within which the manager must work. It is unwise to be over restrictive in setting these, but limits might usefully be set on the more speculative areas such as commodity, exposure and currency dealings. The limits can always be revised at a later stage when a track record has been established. The manager should also provide a detailed management agreement covering their ways of conducting business and restrictions imposed by the client.

The selection process can take up some time but this should be time well spent. It is important to note that many so called financial advisors are purely and simply insurance and investment salesmen. Their interest in the expatriate is high when he has disposable income and wanes immediately that situation ceases. The investments they sell may be perfectly satisfactory but the lack of any ongoing commitment and continuing advice renders them inappropriate to most expatriates.

On the question of charges, these come in a variety of forms. Where the expatriate is purely seeking advice then he should expect to pay for it. Many advisors charge fees on an hourly basis or some form of annual or other periodic retainer. Where investments are placed on behalf of the client a commission is generally paid to the advisor or broker and this may be offset against any hourly or other fee. Many advisors offer a "free" service but this must raise the question of how they are to be remunerated and the obvious answer is solely by commission, ie they are under pressure to sell something. Such "free" services should be considered with a degree of scepticism although this is not to imply that all advisors operating on this basis are less than sound. For investment management there is a further variety of charging structures. There may be a straightforward percentage fee, commonly of the order of ½ to 1 per cent per annum of funds under management and perhaps subject to a minimum annual charge of, say, £250. In addition, most managers will charge for dealing costs. In some cases these fees too may be offset against the commissions received by the managers. Again if the manager is remunerated only by commission the investor should ensure that the managers are not generating cash for themselves by unnecessarily churning the portfolio in order to generate further commissions. Certain investment managers charge performance fees and this should be carefully evaluated and should not come into effect until a certain profit threshold has been reached. When an investment manager has been selected the investor should expect to be given progress reports at least half yearly and preferably more frequently. These reports should show all movements in and out of the portfolio, initial cost of investments and current value. Where the investments are unit trusts or similar investment vehicles the value quoted should be the current bid value — not the offer price or any mid price as these provide a major distortion of the order of three to six per cent. Finally, the investor should allow his manager some time to show his mettle; unless something goes dramatically wrong the manager should have at least two years to prove his worth.

INVESTMENT STRATEGY
One of the most common features I have found in sorting out the financial affairs of expatriates is that their investments comprise a motley collection of unit trusts, offshore funds, insurance policies and so on — some are good, most are adequate and some are downright awful. In most cases these investments have been collected from a variety of brokers, newspaper and magazine advertisements, and whatever the flavour of the month was at any particular time. It is

relatively rare to find a portfolio which has been properly planned from the start and which is designed to meet particular requirements.

Planning a strategy

Firstly it must be understood that there is no single expatriate investment strategy. There are as many potential strategies as there are expatriates. But strategy must be related to an objective and some objectives are common to many expatriates. The sensible way to tackle strategy is first of all to identify these objectives. Commonly expressed aims include the following:

(1)   maximum capital acquisition but without any specific end commitment at this time;
(2)   capital acquisition to fund a particular future commitment such as business or property purchase, school fees, etc;
(3)   capital acquisition to provide or supplement income at the end of the period abroad — either in retirement or simply to provide a better standard of living on a reduced UK salary.

Each of these objectives needs to be considered separately although there may be areas of overlap and certain principles may be common to all strategies.

Having specified his objective the expatriate must then ask himself the following basic questions:

(1)   How much money do I have to invest and how much can I realistically expect to save or invest regularly?
(2)   What minimum timescale is involved — one year, five years, or more?
(3)   What is my attitude to risk — am I very cautious, a speculator or, like most of us, somewhere in between?

In devising any investment strategy account must be taken of three main elements — liquidity, security and growth. In addition, particularly given the volatility of investment markets and currencies, any strategy must retain a large measure of flexibility. This last point may be frustrated by an over-reliance on some types of regular savings plans or an over-indulgence in long term pension planning. Where such contractual saving schemes are used (see later) they should not take up the expatriate's entire disposable income.

Regardless of the expatriate's eventual goal, I would suggest that any investment strategy should be started cautiously with the emphasis on liquidity and security. When a reasonable capital base has been established slightly greater risks can be taken. Only when a substantial investment portfolio has been acquired should the more speculative ventures be considered, and then only for a modest proportion of the expatriate's total worth. For the investor who has visions of wealth through wildcat oil drilling or cornering the market in copper, this may sound like a good basis for boredom. It may well be, but it still makes sense and patience is an essential virtue in any investment venture.

78

Bringing this general strategy down to actual cases, a reasonable plan of campaign might run as follows:

(1)   Initial savings go to form a liquid capital reserve — bank deposit or high interest cheque account in the expatriate's base currency;

(2)   first investment proper goes into a secure pooled fund vehicle such as an offshore gilt, fixed interest, managed currency or Eurobond fund;

(3)   with initial investment of £5,000 or more consider using two or more funds;

(4)   after these funds consider international equity funds with growth rather than income potential — these may be offshore funds or UK authorised unit trusts;

(5)   subsequent savings could be invested in specialist offshore funds with either a geographical bias (investing in North America or Japan, say) or an investment bias (hi-technology, recovery situations, or commodities, for example);

(6)   when capital reaches about £50,000 the investor might usefully consider a portfolio management service to manage existing fund investments and to place new money;

(7)   some small exposure to gold or foreign currencies might also be considered at that point (if not already covered under previous headings);

(8)   investment beyond £100,000 mark may include more speculative items such as individual commodity funds, venture capital schemes and oil developments, but these should be kept to a small proportion of the total portfolio;

(9)   where a portfolio exceeds £150,000 it may be more cost-effective to invest in equities, bonds, etc, directly rather than through the medium of managed funds. At that level it should be possible to achieve a sufficient spread of risk within the portfolio and not rely on the risk spreading advantages of funds or unit trusts. It should be noted, however, that on the one hand many expatriates enter the direct investment arena at a much earlier level and on the other hand, many investment managers will not accept a portfolio for direct investment below £200,000 or £250,000, preferring to stick with a fund portfolio up to that point.

LONG TERM SAVINGS AND PENSIONS

The previously described strategic planning will produce an immediate access directly held portfolio. Such a portfolio if properly managed maintains very high flexibility but can be tailored to any investment aim or eventual commitment. Where there is a specific future commitment the emphasis within the strategic portfolio may be greater on security or some form of guarantee. The basic questions remain the same but with an important addition: is the target required a single fixed sum, a target range or a series of sums at regular intervals?

In this particular area there is no shortage of special savings plans —

the guaranteed mortgage plans, school fee plans, pension plans, etc. Generally speaking these are euphemisms for life assurance policies. That in itself does not put them beyond the pale but the question must be asked, is it necessary to use life assurance? The answer is a resounding no. These plans, however, can be useful and may have a part to play in strategic planning but they are hardly ever the panaceas they are made out to be. It is perfectly reasonable to use a normal directly invested portfolio of the type already described to meet these requirements. If greater emphasis is given to deposits, bond and managed currency funds rather than equity funds, then a reasonably accurate estimate of future returns can be calculated. There remains an element of risk but it is greatly reduced and there is also the possibility of greater growth.

The problem with particular savings plans and guaranteed schemes is that their charges are generally higher than those incurred in direct investment and in the case of specific guarantees, these are either pitched very conservatively or they can have a further cost. So far as any life cover is concerned this can generally be obtained more cheaply by a straightforward level term policy to cover the period concerned. The other major drawback concerns the loss of flexibility. It is all very well having fixed ideas about buying a pub in the village or sending the girls to Roedean, but circumstances do change. Long term commitments can easily become unwanted and unnecessary millstones. That said, many expatriates feel much more secure if they do put aside at least part of their savings for a particular purpose, if not beyond their reach for any other purpose, at least sufficiently difficult to remove without careful thought. In these circumstances some insurance policies may be useful. The points to look for include a relatively short funding period (less than five years), a good performance record with at least minimal guarantees, access to the investment in extremis on demand, preferably by means of policy loans to avoid any early surrender penalties.

The use of such plans for "core planning" is acceptable but they are not recommended for the whole of the expatriate's savings and must never replace the liquidity element of the total portfolio.

Pension planning

Again, any properly structured directly held investment portfolio can provide a pension which, after all, is only a stream of income. However, in this area it may be more appropriate than elsewhere to look at what the regular or contractual savings plans have to offer.

Many offshore insurance companies offer "expatriate pension plans" but it must be remembered that these are not directly analogous to UK pension plans. In the main they are non-qualifying life policies and the proceeds if taken when the policyholder is resident in the UK will attract tax. Where the investor is likely to spend a substantial period overseas or if he expects to retire outside the UK then these plans may be particularly appropriate. Where the overseas period, however, is unlikely to exceed say five years then such plans are unlikely to be tax efficient unless they can be exchanged for a similar UK insurance policy following the expatriate's return. Briefly the way such offshore policies are now taxed is that the proceeds are apportioned between the period of non-residence and the total period during which the investment has been held and the proportion equal to the UK resident period is liable for UK tax and no credit is given for tax at the basic rate (as would be the case with a UK policy). Thus, for example, a policy taken out in 1985 by an expatriate returning to the UK in 1990 would have five years of non-resident and non-taxable profit. If the proceeds were taken as an annual income from 1995 the first year's income would be 50 per cent taxable, the income in 1996 would be 6/11th's taxable, in 1997 7/12th's, etc.

In this area of long term planning it is essential that proper professional advice is taken to identify the most appropriate product in the circumstances.

Finally, it must be noted that UK personal pension plans are generally not available to expatriates. It happens not infrequently that expatriates, perhaps at home on leave, consult their UK insurance broker and either through his own lack of knowledge or because the client does not give him all the information, the client may be sold a UK personal pension plan. These plans are exempt from UK income and capital gains taxes but in order to retain this exemption the funds invested in them must come from UK "relevant income". Relevant income comes from employment or self-employment in the UK and in the former case only from an employment where there is no company pension scheme applicable. Your salary from Wonderful Gulf Industries Ltd will not qualify. The insurance company risks losing its exempt status within its pension plan if non-relevant income is accepted. Any expatriate in this position should inform the insurance company concerned of all the facts and, in most cases, the investment will be refunded.

OFFSHORE FUNDS

The offshore fund industry is often considered as the expatriate's equivalent of the domestic UK unit trust industry. In some respects this is a fair comparison in that both are pooling devices for investors and thus, theoretically, the single investor's risk is minimised by a broad spread of investment. Some offshore funds are, indeed, unit trusts, others are open-ended investment companies but the overall effect is similar. Offshore funds are very largely aimed at the expatriate community and they do offer a wide range of investment areas without the tax problems which sometimes attach to UK investments. However, the expatriate should not totally disregard UK unit trusts. Where investment for capital growth is concerned there is little to choose between offshore funds and unit trusts. Where the investment however generates a high income offshore funds are generally to be preferred. These funds are invariably established in countries with either little or no taxation and the income return can be made gross. Thus, funds investing in gilts, monetary instruments and Eurobonds can pay the investor without deduction of any tax. Gilt unit trusts in the UK pay dividends effectively net of tax, ie with a tax credit. The charging structure of offshore funds and authorised unit trusts is generally similar although offshore funds may, on average, charge slightly more.

Apart from gross income, the offshore funds do offer other advantages. The range of investment areas open to the offshore fund manager is much wider than that available to the domestic unit trust. Unit trusts in the UK are strictly regulated by the Department of Trade and Industry and they are forbidden to hold commodities, or more than a small proportion of investment in unlisted companies, or property. Offshore funds are not so restricted (note, the UK unit trust industry may be, partly at least, deregulated over the next year or so). In addition to the wider investment field, offshore funds also provide a range of currency exposure. UK unit trusts are all denominated in sterling regardless of the underlying investments. Offshore funds are available denominated in all the major currencies and commonly in the currency of the main investment area. Thus, funds investing in the Far East will often be quoted in yen or Hong Kong dollars, European investing funds may be in Swiss francs, Deutschmarks, etc, American specialist funds and many commodity funds are quoted in US dollars and so on. As well as currency exposure in this way there are other offshore funds which invest specifically in foreign currency, either on deposit or through government bonds and other monetary instruments. These funds are available either on a managed basis, where the fund managers decide the currency mix, or on an individual currency basis where the decision as to which currency to choose is left to the individual investor. These funds are not available as UK unit trusts.

Following the 1984 Finance Act offshore funds fall into one of two categories — those with distributor status and those without. Funds without distributor status are to be avoided by expatriates unless they are confident that their overseas stay will last for some lengthy period or that they will only sell their investment in a subsequent period of non-residence. The reason for this is that non-distributor funds are subject to income tax on disposal on both income and capital growth. Funds which have distributor status will be taxed in the normal way, ie income tax on any distributions made and capital gains tax if appropriate on the eventual sale. (In both cases it is assumed the investor is UK resident at the appropriate time.) In order to qualify for distributor status the fund manager must apply to the Inland Revenue each year and they will be accepted only where they can show that substantially all income produced by the fund and not absorbed in management charges, etc, has been distributed in the form of dividend to the investors. Many investors do not wish to receive income while they are working abroad and, in many cases, the dividends themselves may be relatively small. Most funds have a reinvestment facility which can avoid this particular problem. Returning expatriates should note, however, that even where dividends are being reinvested they will have to account for these dividends in their UK tax returns and pay income tax accordingly.

Umbrella funds

This represents a recent innovation in the offshore fund market. Many offshore fund management groups have for many years offered a wide range of either country or regional specific funds or funds in specific investment areas. Many groups also offered a portfolio management service involving these funds. For the returned expatriate, however, switching from fund to fund even within the same group involved a potential capital gains tax liability on each switch. With these umbrella funds this tax consideration no longer applies. An umbrella fund is treated as a single fund with a variety of sub-funds which may cover all investment areas and regions. Switching from sub-fund to sub-fund need not constitute a disposal for capital gains tax purposes so portfolio management can be carried out without constraint. Where the investor, however, wishes to realise a gain, perhaps within his annual exemption limit in order to increase his purchase price against any future disposal, such funds can be bed and breakfasted in the normal way. Funds of this type are available from some of the major offshore fund management groups including Wardley, Gartmore, Guinness Flight and several others.

Fund management groups and broker funds
Most of the major UK trust companies and banks also operate offshore funds. Funds are, however, also provided by many other overseas financial institutions and many of these are highly respectable and provide excellent investment opportunities. However, in some cases and in some locations regulation of fund managers leaves much to be desired and the expatriate should show a degree of caution in dealing with any unfamiliar manager or management group.

Many financial advisors also operate their own unit trusts or offshore funds which may be either directly invested in equities, bonds, or whatever, or they may be funds of funds. The security of these funds obviously depends on regulation and where the funds are UK based or based in reputable areas such as the Channel Islands or the Isle of Man they may be considered relatively safe. The performance of the funds will be determined by the advisor's own ability in this area and some are extremely good. A fund of funds can in some respects be considered as a convenient form of portfolio management which, like umbrella funds, allows the investor to have constantly changing exposure to different markets without incurring any immediate tax liability. The watchword, however, must remain caution but where a financial advisor has been satisfactorily managing a portfolio of funds on your behalf then his own broker fund or fund of funds should be equally satisfactory.

OTHER INVESTMENTS
In many countries with sophisticated financial markets expatriates may wish to indulge in the local investment scene. Again, unless they are experienced investors they would do well to take local advice.

Other local "investments" such as carpets, antiques, works of art, jewellery, etc, may also have a part to play, but these should rarely be of more than relatively minor significance to an overall financial strategy.

Finally, property as an investment is little different from any other investment medium in that it can be good, bad or anywhere in the middle. The major drawback to property is that it can be a very illiquid investment and disposal can present on occasion certain problems. Apart from purchasing property directly (with or without a mortgage) exposure to the market can be obtained through some offshore funds and many life assurance funds. These may be preferable to the actual bricks and mortar, at least for the smaller investor.

TAKE OUR ADVICE AND SAVE MONEY

Any advice that saves you money must be good advice.

And how to get it can be found in our Financial Advice for British Expatriates booklet.

For your copy just complete the coupon and send it to the address below:

Name_____

Address_____

WA

EXPATRIATE ADVISORY SERVICES PLC
14 Gordon Road, West Bridgford, Nottingham NG2 5LN Tel (0602) 816572/816897 Telex 377801 Expat G Fax (0602) 455076

6

UK property

Property has often been described as the expatriate's best investment and there are arguments both for and against this view. In this chapter, I shall be considering the expatriate's own home. If he owns a property before he goes abroad he will have various options open to him, if he wishes to buy while overseas there are special schemes to help, and in each case there are tax, legal, and financial considerations to be taken into account.

IF YOU ALREADY OWN A PROPERTY

Options for existing property

One of the first things an expatriate has to decide when he is posted abroad with his family is what to do about the family home. He can either sell it or retain it. If he retains it, he can either leave it standing empty or he can rent it out. Whichever course he follows will be dictated by his own philosophy. He may want no hassle at all while he is abroad, so he will sell it; or perhaps he does want to keep it but feels less than happy about strangers using his home, so he will leave it vacant; or he may see his home as a useful source of income, possibly enough to pay the mortgage, so he lets it. Each of these alternatives comes complete with its own set of problems.

Anyone who has ever sold property in the UK knows just how unpredictable a process it is. While recent years have seen a generally buoyant housing market this has not been evenly spread throughout the country. In the south-east of England, parts of the West Country and East·Anglia and around some of the major cities elsewhere in the UK the demand for property has remained very high. But even in these locations certain properties in certain parts can stick on the market for months. For someone who is about to leave the country this can cause obvious difficulty. The alternatives then are to accept a much lower price in order to complete the sale in good time — and even by so doing there are no guarantees — or to leave an estate agent and solicitor in charge. Awkward as this is, it is not the major drawback to selling up. That comes on the eventual return to the UK when a new property is sought. Historically, house prices have risen faster than the rate of inflation, and this has certainly been the case over the last few years. However, the major price rises have been primarily in those areas mentioned above and in other parts of the country the market is much more depressed both in terms of movement and price. What can happen, particularly in the better areas, is that the returning expatriate finds that even to repurchase the house he sold some years earlier will cost him far more than the capital he has saved in the interim.

The second option for the expatriate is to leave his house empty. There are two advantages to this: firstly, the expatriate retains his place on the housing ladder, and secondly, he will have a home base for UK holidays. This second advantage, however, must be tempered with the warning about available accommodation and its effect on non-working expatriates (see chapter 3 — **Taxation**).

The greatest drawback to leaving property vacant is the British climate and weather. Floods, high winds, lightning and subsidence take their toll of many houses each year. It is essential that the house insurance is checked before leaving to ensure that all of these hazards are covered when the property is unoccupied for long periods. The insurers should be told and the additional premiums necessary should be paid. As one expatriate in Oman found out, the extra premium was well worth paying: his property suffered from a burst pipe in early 1982 and the havoc caused in the three days before it was discovered cost £14,000 to put right. His insurers, who had charged him an extra £80 per annum, paid up. The other major risk to unoccupied property is that of break-in, vandalism or squatters. No house can be made impregnable to a determined intruder but the owner can provide as much discouragement as possible through fitting secure locks to all doors and windows (this might also be a term of the insurance policy). All utilities should be disconnected and such things as oil tanks and coal cellars should be emptied. It is assumed that valuable items not being taken abroad will be put into secure storage or left with relatives, but general household contents insurance should also be checked and any amended premium paid.

The final problem associated with leaving the house empty can come from the bank or building society if the house is being bought on a mortgage. Most mortgage agreements contain a clause to the effect that the property will not be left vacant other than for normal holiday periods without the express permission of the mortgagee. This permission is only rarely withheld but many lenders ask for a higher rate of interest on the mortgage for the unoccupied period.

The expatriate's best defence against most of the risks outlined above is a trusted and accommodating neighbour or relative. This person should keep a regular and close eye on the property, should have the expatriate's solicitor's name and address and should be able to act through the solicitor or independently in the event of any major problem. Finally, a set of house keys should be left at the local police station.

The third option for the expatriate home owner is to become an absentee landlord. This, wherever feasible, is the recommended option for most expatriates. It is also the one most fraught with worries both justified and unjustified. Mainly these worries involve regaining possession, the trustworthiness of tenants, and taxation. However, if the proper procedures are carried out these problems can be put into the proper perspective and can generally be handled without too much trouble.

The right to repossession

This can be ensured in one of two ways. The first involves a special type of lease known as 'shorthold' which can be granted for a fixed period of from one to five years, at the end of which the tenant is obliged to move out. The second and commoner method is by means of a 'Case 11 notice'. This is a notice which incorporates a clause stating that the landlord is an owner-occupier within the meaning of the Rent Act 1977. It should also state that he or she will require possession for personal occupation at the end of the tenancy and is entitled to that possession under Case 11 of Schedule 15 to that Act. This notice should be specifically acknowledged by the tenant before or at the same time as the tenancy agreement is signed. It is not necessary to specify at what date repossession will be required, notice to quit can be served at any time, but the minimum notice period is four weeks or the period for which rent is collected, whichever is the greater; thus, if rent is payable quarterly, three months would be the minimum notice period. The 1977 Act required that the owner actually returned to the property and physically occupied it but this was waived under the Rent Act 1980 where the owner could prove that he needed a property nearer to his place of employment. Thus the expatriate with a house in Liverpool who is returning to a job in Manchester could claim he must move to Manchester and so regain possession of his property. Whether he does, in fact, move house to Manchester will not affect his claim.

However, it is all very well having these two types of tenancies but tenants might still stay put. The answer then is to have them legally evicted. This process can take up to three months but normally averages about three to six weeks. The prudent landlord will allow for this possibility and will aim to terminate the tenancy a month or so before he expects to take possession. The rent forgone may be much less than any hotel expenses incurred while awaiting the due process of law. Legal expenses insurance is also quite cheap and is available for most tenancy and repossession suits.

In the most recent Queen's Speech the government indicated that they are to re-examine the Rent Act and the provision of rented accommodation in the UK. This is likely to result in fewer restrictions placed on landlords and perhaps easier repossession. Details of such changes must, obviously, await the next edition of this book. However, it cannot be stressed enough that anyone contemplating entering into a leasing agreement must use the specialist services of a solicitor and it is to be expected that such solicitors will themselves be *au fait* with all new developments.

Agents and tenants

Estate agents and property managers come in all shapes and sizes, the good, the bad, and the adequate. The best one is the one who comes with a personal recommendation based on satisfactory past experience. A good agent is worth his weight in rent and certainly the 10–15 per cent he will charge. The services he should provide include: selection of tenants, collection of rents and initial deposits, payment of bills such as rates and insurance, regular inspection of the property and instituting any necessary repairs (with a predetermined cost limit for reference to the landlord), preparation of accounts and payment of any income tax due.

As do agents, tenants too come in all shapes and sizes. In theory at least, the best tenant to have is a company or institution such as a university (specify no students). Such a tenant will use the property for visiting staff or as temporary accommodation for new staff. Apart from being reasonably secure payers and generally prepared to pay for any dilapidation, a company or similar tenant will have no security of tenure. In most cases, however, the selection of tenants will be left to the agent or the expatriate's solicitor.

UK PROPERTY AND TAXATION

Of greatest interest to the expatriate landlord is his liability to income tax and capital gains tax and any tax relief available for mortgage interest.

Income tax

Income tax chargeable

Where property is let, the rent is chargeable to income tax regardless of the residence status of the landlord. Rental income can be charged under either of two tax Schedules depending on whether the property is let furnished or unfurnished.

Unfurnished letting is assessed under Schedule A to the Income and Corporation Taxes Act 1970 and the assessment is normally made on the net income taxable in the previous year. Where the actual income for the current year is different, an adjustment will be made to the initial assessment in due course. For example: the 1987/88 assessment will charge tax on the net income received in 1986/87. This tax is normally due on 1st January 1988. If, at the end of the tax year, the net income is less than the amount assessed (and paid before the tax year end), a repayment will be made. Similarly, if the net income for 1987/88 is greater than the original assessment, a further assessment will be issued. The only time the overpayment/repayment syndrome can be challenged is where the property is disposed of before the tax due date, i.e. 1st January.

Furnished letting is assessed under Case VI of Schedule D to the Income and Corporation Taxes Act 1970 and the amount assessed is the actual net income in the year of assessment. The assessment will be raised and tax will be payable in the same way as Schedule A assessments but in this case the landlord can appeal against and postpone tax charged on the amount assessed if it appears excessive; alternatively the assessment may not be raised until after the end of the tax year concerned when proper accounts have been submitted.

So much for the basis of assessment. For expatriate landlords there is a further complication. If the tenant pays the rent directly to the non-resident landlord, he is required to deduct tax at the basic rate, currently 27 per cent, from the gross payment and account for that tax to the Inland Revenue. It is then up to the landlord to make a claim for any allowable deductions (see below). But, if the landlord employs a managing agent, the tenant can pay the gross rent to the agent who will then prepare proper accounts, including deductions, and pay the tax due on the net income. The agent is wholly responsible for the tax payable and it is up to him to retain sufficient of the rent to pay this liability. But a good agent knowing the likely net assessable income should not need to retain a full 27 per cent of the rent, so compared with the direct payment from the tenant the use of an agent should improve the expatriate's cash flow.

The landlord can deduct many necessary expenses from his gross income to arrive at the taxable amount. These include current repairs and redecoration inside and outside the property, but not to the extent of materially improving, altering, or extending the property. Thus the cost of replacement of rotting windows will be allowed but not if the replacement involves complete double glazing, for example. Other major deductions include:

(1) insurance premiums against damage to the fabric of the property;
(2) valuation fees for insurance purposes;
(3) legal and accountancy costs for preparation of accounts, etc.;
(4) managing agent's fees;
(5) local authority rates unless paid directly by the tenants;
(6) an allowance for depreciation of furniture and fittings (generally 10 per cent of rent less any rates paid by the landlord); and
(7) mortgage interest relief (see below).

89

Tax relief for mortgage interest

Of the several deductions listed above the one of greatest importance to most expatriates is the mortgage interest relief. Where the basic condition that the lender or mortgagee is resident in the UK or is a branch of a UK bank situated in the Channel Islands is met, then relief can be given in one of two ways. Firstly, on loans up to £30,000, or on the first £30,000 of larger loans, the MIRAS scheme may be operated. MIRAS (Mortgage Interest Relief At Source) was introduced in 1983 and is analagous to the way in which life assurance premium relief was given prior to its abolition. That is, the borrower pays interest to the lender net of tax at the basic rate with the shortfall being made up to the lender by the Inland Revenue in due course. Strictly, therefore, if the monthly interest element on a mortgage repayment was £350, the payment actually made by the borrower would be £255.50 (assuming the loan was for no more than £30,000). This would, in fact, be the amount payable if the mortgage was an endowment mortgage or (although not applicable to most expatriates) a mortgage being repaid by means of a pension plan. For the traditional capital repayment mortgage there would be a capital element added to the £255.50 plus, in most cases, an adjustment to spread the interest over the full period of the mortgage. With this traditional mortgage repayment method the tax relief declines as the outstanding mortgage decreases and most building societies, for their convenience, take account of this and spread the relief evenly. The net result is a higher mortgage payment than that strictly required under the rules in the early years with greater relief being given at the latter part of the mortgage period.

To quality for tax relief under the MIRAS scheme the property concerned must either be the borrower's only or main residence or that of his or his spouse's dependent relative (in which the case the property must be provided rent free and without other consideration), or, finally, the only or main residence of the borrower's separated or former spouse. Obviously, for expatriates the UK property will not be the only residence nor, in most cases, will it be the main residence. However, relief can still be given under an extra-statutory concession which is described more fully later — see Tax and Unlet Property. Where the expatriate has been receiving relief under MIRAS before going abroad then the relief may continue to be given in the same way following his departure (subject to his meeting the necessary conditions of the concession mentioned above). Where interest is paid under the MIRAS scheme it cannot be used to offset the rental profit — this would involve double relief. Where the rent, net of other expenses, is quite small and less than the amount of interest actually paid MIRAS operates to the expatriate's advantage. But where the rental income is large and the mortgage is greater than £30,000 the alternative form of relief is far superior.

This alternative route to relief can only be given where the property concerned is let at a commercial rent for more than 26 weeks in any 52 week period and when not so let is either available for letting or is being used as the only or main residence of the landlord or is prevented from being available because of repair or construction work. In these cases there is no upper limit to the amount of mortgage interest which can be relieved subject only to relief being given against rental income. Any surplus of relief can be carried forward for use against rental income in subsequent years. The following examples illustrate the two ways in which relief can be given:

Example 1

Mortgage £30,000 @ 11% pa. Rent (excluding rates) £250 per month.

    (a) MIRAS applies   Interest paid in year = £2,409

Rent	£3,000
Expenses, say	£1,000
Taxable Profit	£2,000
Income tax	540
Net return	£1,460

        Net cost to borrower £949

    (b) MIRAS not applied   Interest paid in year = £3,300

Rent	£3,000	
Expenses	£1,000	
	£2,000	
Interest	3,300	
Tax loss	(£1,300)	carried forward to subsequent years
Income tax	nil	
Net return	(£2,000)	[ie rent net of expenses]

        Net cost to borrower £1,300

        Saving if MIRAS applies £351

Example 2

Mortgage £60,000 @ 11% pa. Rent (excluding rates) £750 per month.

(a) MIRAS applies   Interest paid in year = £5,709
(MIRAS applied only to £30,000)

Rent	£9,000
Expenses	£2,000
Profit	£7,000
Tax payable	1,890
Net return	£5,110

Net cost to borrower £599

(b) MIRAS not applied   Interest paid in year = £6,600

Rent	£9,000
Expenses	£2,000
	£7,000
Interest	6,600
Profit	£400
Tax payable	108
	£292

Net profit to borrower £292

Saving if MIRAS **not** applied £891

Where the expatriate owns several properties all of which are rented out then the tax computation can be made on the total figures. In this way a rent surplus on one property can be reduced by a surplus of relief perhaps on another. This, however, brings us more into the realms of investment than the family home and this aspect is discussed more fully in chapter 5.

Tax and unlet property
Expatriates will no doubt be relieved to know that where they are not generating an income they have no income tax to pay. They may still, however, qualify for tax relief against their mortgage interest. For most expatriates the greatest measure of relief will be through the MIRAS system and the conditions necessary to qualify for this relief are discussed below.

Prior to April 1983 a UK resident who was not liable to tax could effectively obtain mortgage interest relief by applying for an "option mortgage". Under this scheme the mortgage repayments were reduced and the balance made up to the lender by the government. The reduction was approximately the amount which would have been available as basic rate tax relief. The option mortgage scheme was discontinued from April 1983 with the introduction of MIRAS. Where the MIRAS mortgagor is a non-taxpayer he still benefits from net payment in the same way as under the option mortgage scheme. Most expatriates are non-taxpayers but whereas they could not obtain an option mortgage they may be entitled to relief under MIRAS. So long as the other conditions for relief are met then whether or not the claimant has UK income is irrelevant as is his or her residence status. Much confusion was obvious when the MIRAS system came into effect in 1983 with many lenders themselves being unsure of the rules and some tax offices being less than helpful. As a consequence many mortgagors who should have benefited, including many expatriates, did not. Since 1983 the situation has been effectively clarified and, perhaps as a result of the many newspaper and magazine articles on MIRAS, many more expatriates are now benefiting. Indeed, in many cases where MIRAS should have been operated but was not, the mortgagors have received a cash repayment for the relief to which they were entitled — and this in some cases where no actual tax had been paid by the mortgagor for several years. I very much doubt whether it was the Government's intention to give such a measure of relief to non-residents but subsequent Finance Acts have failed to remove what must be seen as an anomaly. On the other hand, the extra-statutory concession on which expatriates rely for this relief has been tightened and its application is no longer as easy as was the case some years ago.

As mentioned earlier, the most important qualification for relief is that the property is the claimant's only or principal private residence. Under the extra-statutory concession this qualification is not lost in the case of temporary absences up to one year. In addition, in the case of a person who is required, by reason of his employment, to move from his home to another place in the UK or abroad, absences of up to four years will not affect his right to relief. This is conditional on the period of absence not being expected to exceed four years and that the property was occupied as the sole or main residence for at least three months prior to the absence and can reasonably be expected to be so used again on return. Relief can, in fact, continue indefinitely so long as the property is reoccupied for at least three months every four years, but if the initial work contract is for five years, it would be to the expatriate's advantage to rearrange this perhaps to a four year contract with an option to continue for a further year. In that way the expectation condition above can be met. Where relief is to continue beyond four years the three months occupancy can cause some problems. It used to be thought that occupation of the property by the borrower's spouse for the three month period would be sufficient. This is one of the areas in which the Revenue have tightened the concession. Occupation of the property must now be by the borrower and, in the case of joint borrowers, by both of them. Unless the expatriate is in the fortunate position of having three months leave available he will lose his MIRAS entitlement. He should also bear in mind that by spending three months in the UK he may be coming close to jeopardising his residence position on the basis of the visit rules. In years gone by the Revenue would also accept that the property was the main residence if it was occupied frequently by the expatriate's family, perhaps on several home leaves coinciding with school holidays, etc. This is no longer acceptable unless the family spend the greater part of the year — not defined but implied over six months — in the property.

Relief under MIRAS for at least four years is not difficult for those expatriates owning the property concerned prior to leaving the UK. The situation is somewhat more difficult for the expatriate who buys a property during his period of overseas working. Again there is the requirement that the property is occupied by the borrower for a period of at least three months and once again, occupation by spouse or family is not in itself sufficient. One possible way around this problem where the wife could occupy the property and her spouse could not is for the wife herself to be the borrower. Assuming that she does not herself have sufficient income to justify such a loan it will be necessary for the husband to act as guarantor but this should present little difficulty.

Initially, MIRAS was only available on loans up to £25,000. This was changed in 1984 to £30,000 and certain lenders were prepared to split larger mortgages so that the £30,000 was eligible for relief and the balance in the form of a second loan was payable gross. Since April 1987 the first £30,000 of any loan is now automatically potentially eligible for MIRAS. Application for MIRAS treatment should be made in the first instance to the lender. The borrower will then receive a form which must be completed and sent to his tax office. Most expatriates however do not have a current tax office and this has sometimes been seen as a block on the claim. This is not so as under these circumstances the form should be forwarded to the Central Unit (MIRAS), 1st Floor, St John's House, Merton Road, Bootle, Merseyside, L69 9BB, where the particular circumstances of the case will be assessed.

Second mortgages

A common way of raising extra cash is to take out a second mortgage or to re-negotiate an existing mortgage with the same or another lender for a higher sum. Interest on the new loan is often allowed by the Inland Revenue in full. This can be a mistake. The interest on the extra sum is only allowable where the new loan is applied for a qualifying purpose, normally purchasing, improving, or developing land which satisfies the conditions already described. Loans applied to central heating, double glazing, a new garage and other such improvements will qualify but a loan applied to buying a new car or a round the world air ticket will not.

Capital gains tax

For most expatriates owning a single property in the UK is unlikely to cause any great problem with capital gains tax. This results from the wide-ranging exemption granted to an individual's sole or main residence.

The exemption is granted as follows: On a dwelling house which has been the individual's sole or main residence throughout his ownership of it (except for all or any part of the last 24 months and temporary absences as detailed below). The exemption also applies to land up to one acre used for the individual's enjoyment and occupation of the residence. A larger land area may be exempt if it is in keeping with the size and character of the property. Temporary periods of absence from the property which do not disturb the capital gains tax exemption are:

(1)   any period or periods not exceeding three years in total; and
(2)   any period throughout which the individual was employed abroad and all the duties of the employment were carried out outside the UK; and
(3)   a period or periods not exceeding four years in total during which the individual was prevented from residing in the property by reason of the location of his work.

Both before and after these periods of absence the property must be the individual's only or main residence except where, after a period of absence, the owner is required to live elsewhere because of his employment.

Unlike the eligibility of mortgage interest relief there is no specified qualifying period during which the property must be occupied but, as with many aspects of tax, a test of reasonableness will give fair guidelines. In this case I would recommend a minimum of one week's physical occupation of the property.

A second property can also be exempt from capital gains tax if it is the sole residence of the owner's dependent relative or the dependent relative of the owner's spouse and the property is occupied rent free. No individual or married couple can have more than two exempt properties.

It is interesting to note, however, that an individual can have two completely separate sole or main residences — one for the purposes of obtaining tax relief on his mortgage and a second for the purposes of capital gains tax exemption. For capital gains tax purposes where two or more properties are owned the owner must elect which one is to be treated as his main residence. This is an elective choice and need not, in fact, signify that it is so used. This little anomaly can be used to advantage in tax planning — in some cases to major advantage. Failure to make the capital gains tax election within two years of acquiring the second property, however, will result in the tax inspector making his own decision as to which property should be exempt. The inspector's decision is unlikely to take into account your tax planning requirements and, while his decision may be subject to appeal, the Appeal Commissioners are unlikely to be swayed by your tax avoiding intentions. The answer is, obviously, to make the election in good time within the two year limit.

Where a property is let it does not normally qualify for exemption. In the case of a sole or main residence let for a period of years the exemption will be restricted by the proportion of the whole period which corresponds to the period let. This will not, however, apply to letting during the owner's absence abroad so long as he occupies the property before and afterwards. Where a capital gains tax charge arises the gain is that made from the date of purchase to the date of sale (subject to any indexation relief) or the gain from 5th April 1965 if the property was owned at or before that time. Where property was owned prior to 5th April 1965 then any gain is apportioned on a straight line basis to show the pre-April '65 gain and the post-April '65 gain, the latter being chargeable. Alternatively, the gain chargeable can be computed from an agreed valuation of the property at 5th April 1965 but given the substantial rise in property prices over the last 22 years it is rare that such a method will be to the individual's advantage.

EARLY REPAYMENT OF MORTGAGES

Many expatriates use capital acquired overseas to repay an existing mortgage. For some, doing this is the raison d'etre of working abroad in the first place. In many cases such a move is wasteful of resources and, on occasion, the right move might be to increase borrowing rather than reduce it. There are several points to be considered. The first concerns the opportunity cost. By this is meant, can the expatriate obtain a higher rate of return on his surplus cash than the interest charged on his mortgage? If he is entitled to mortgage interest relief (under MIRAS or against letting income) the answer is probably yes because he can invest tax free. If he has no entitlement to this tax relief, then it may be more difficult to obtain a guaranteed better return but, in that case, he might look at the second consideration — flexibility. If he can obtain the same return as his interest rate on the mortgage he will be in a no gain/no loss position as regards his money but money repaid to the building society is effectively locked into his property whereas money invested elsewhere will remain available for any contingencies. The only time it is advisable to repay a mortgage early is on a standard repayment mortgage which has only a few years (up to five) to run. In the final few years of repayment the true rate of interest is much higher than the nominal rate because of the way most societies calculate it. In these circumstances early repayment can have a significant advantage.

BUYING WHILE OVERSEAS

When it comes to lending to expatriates, a building society welcome is often notable by its absence. But finding a mortgage is only one, although often the greatest, of the headaches of the expatriate house buyer. The first problem comes in actually finding the property to buy.

Finding a property

Most expatriates have only a limited time in which to find the house they want; usually the search is confined to two or three months of home leave perhaps preceded by requests for property details from the appropriate estate agents in the preferred locality. But even if the potential buyer knows just what he wants, when he wants it, where,

96

and how much he can afford, it can still take an inordinate length of time to find. Estate agents are not renowned for sticking to a detailed brief, they tend to inform prospective buyers of almost everything on their books.

Apart from a personal house search the expatriate may be able to find his property with the aid of one of the property search companies which have become established in recent years. Unlike an estate agent a property search company works for the purchaser not the seller. In theory, at least, the property search company will stick closely to a client brief and will send comprehensive details to the client only of the most suitable properties.

In addition to finding appropriate property, these companies will also obtain survey reports, negotiate on price, and engage solicitors. The expatriate buyer can, if he wishes, leave the entire process to the company and many do, especially if the property is intended as an investment rather than as a permanent home. Charges for this sort of service vary but somewhere in the region of 2–3 per cent would be normal.

Many property search companies as well as other estate agencies operate as property managers. As has been mentioned earlier, property managers are as variable as tenants and it pays to look around and find out, if at all possible, from other expatriates those who have proved to be useful.

Raising the money

Having found a property the next step is to obtain a mortgage. As already mentioned, the general attitude of building societies to expatriate borrowers has often been less than helpful. Although few societies will admit to refusing to consider a mortgage application from an expatriate, such borrowers rate very low on the societies' list of priorities. Some societies will be reasonably sympathetic to expatriates who intend to return to the UK within twelve months, but where the anticipated return is three or more years away, fewer than one in five societies will be interested. Where the expatriate's family intend to occupy the property, more favourable consideration can be expected but this concession is of little use to the single expatriate or the expatriate family who prefer to stay together.

A further disincentive for the expatriate is the near certainty that he will have to pay more for his mortgage than the UK resident borrower. Although the Building Societies Association declares a recommended rate for lending the individual societies are not bound by it. Rarely will any offer to lend at a lower rate than the recommended one but some will charge more and for some mortgages it may be much more. Smaller societies commonly charge ¼–½ per cent over the recommended rate for any mortgage; most societies charge extra interest on a sliding scale depending on the size of the mortgage — an extra ½ per cent for loans between £15,000 and £20,000, more for loans up to £25,000 and perhaps as much as 2 per cent more for loans over £30,000. The perfectly reasonable, say, 10 per cent recommended rate can soon be left far behind, with a large loan from a small society costing perhaps 13 per cent. For the expatriate that is not the end of the story. If he is able to obtain a loan at all he is likely to find an extra charge of 1 per cent and if he obtains permission to let the property this can be doubled.

In the last few years, however, things have started to look up for the expatriate borrower. Several societies are now offering special schemes for expatriates involving either a mortgage guarantee in return for regular savings lasting one to three years, or the promise of high priority for a loan, again after a period of saving.

But building societies are not the only sources of mortgage finance. The clearing banks in the last few years have entered the mortgage market in a big way and on several occasions have undercut the building society interest rates. Interest rates apart, where bank funds are available they will often be given in greater quantity. Building society loans in excess of £45,000 are the exception but the banks are much more prepared to give loans in the £45,000 to £100,000 range. And unlike the building societies, the banks are also likely to reduce the interest rate on a large loan, rather than increase it.

In recent years many other organisations have come into the mortgage business. Apart from the secondary banks, finance companies and insurance companies there are now several pure mortgage organisations who often offer the most competitive terms both for UK residents and expatriates. In the main, these latest entrants to the mortgage field are looking to the future when mortgages can be securitised, ie mortgage debt can be traded in much the same way as government debt is traded on the gilt market. Such a secondary mortgage market already exists in the US and in some other countries, and it is perhaps only a matter of time before this becomes well established in the UK. For the actual borrower this should not make any significant difference to the terms of his borrowing. One effect of the new borrowing scene is that there is an added dynamism to the whole lending market. Almost exclusively companies such as National Home Loans and the Mortgage Corporation are involved in endowment or pension mortgages under which the whole mortgage remains outstanding to the end of its term, the only payment made to the lender being the interest due. The loan is repaid from the proceeds of the endowment or pension policy at maturity and, depending on the insurance company's performance, there may also be an additional sum available beyond what is required to pay off the loan (it is also quite possible that the sum available will be insufficient — hence the need to pick your insurance company carefully). Also very much involved in the endowment and pension mortgage scene are the insurance companies themselves — for obvious reasons. Until quite recently most insurance companies would only become involved on a "top up" basis under which they would perhaps lend an additional 20 per cent of the purchase price where the purchaser had already arranged say a 75 per cent mortgage with a bank or building society. Today, some of the major insurance companies including those with offshore offshoots are now quite willing to lend to expatriates.

Whether or not an endowment or pension mortgage is appropriate for the expatriate is, in some cases, a moot point. Firstly, on the pension front mortgages are only available against personal UK authorised pension plans. Expatriates, as described in chapter 5, do not qualify, as a rule, for such plans. They can, however, take out an endowment insurance policy and are frequently urged to do so. In gross terms the repayment mortgage is almost always cheaper than the endowment mortgage but the last year or two have seen more competitive insurance packages being presented and, assuming the estimates on which maturity proceeds are based are adequately conservative, they now represent from most companies good value. This is particularly so in the case of relatively young expatriates (certainly those under age 35) but with increasing age the cost of the life assurance cover naturally increases. A further point to bear in mind is that if the mortgage is likely to be repaid early, to obtain maximum benefit from the endowment policy the premiums must be continued to the end, or close to the end, of the original period. If the mortgage is redeemed and another mortgage on a new property taken out most policies from the more reputable companies can be transferred and, where there is a shortfall in cover, an additional policy taken out. There is rarely any need for an original policy to be cancelled and a new policy taken out for the entirety of the new mortgage. Such practice from insurance and mortgage brokers is not unknown and anyone faced with that situation should look elsewhere.

Finally, a word of warning may be appropriate following on from my last statement. Beware the insurance broker who claims that by taking out a long term policy immediately, a mortgage several years hence in the UK will be a mere formality. It will not. It is never a mere formality even if, with some few policies and even fewer brokers, a mortgage does become available. Brokers and lenders are much more likely to find a first mortgage to coincide with a first premium of a policy than the fiftieth premium. Generally speaking offshore life assurance contracts are not suitable and are commonly rejected as collateral by UK lenders. There are exceptions but sound professional advice should be sought before following this route.

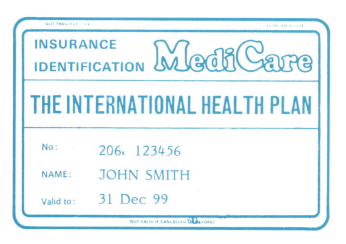

7

Family matters

THE EXPATRIATE WIFE

The secret of expatriate success from the wife's point of view was put to me thus by a very experienced expatriate lady in Riyadh: 'Be a joiner. Joiners will have a good time and benefit from their stay abroad. The loner will often be miserable and make expatriate life impossible for the whole family.' While these uncompromising remarks are perhaps an overstatement there is much truth in them, particularly for the expatriate wife in the third world or in countries whose culture is far removed from Western society. Loneliness can be the most serious drawback to expatriate life and the person who does not make friends easily can be at a distinct disadvantage.

One of the first things a potential expatriate wife should do is make sure she is involved with her husband from the start. Most enlightened expatriate employers are aware of the importance of a contented expatriate family and will make the effort to reassure a wife and provide her with ample background information and, with the best companies, will ensure that she attends any briefing conferences or courses with her husband. The courses run by the Centre for International Briefing at Farnham Castle in Surrey are regularly attended by husbands and wives and the feedback the Centre receives shows how beneficial this is. These briefings last four days and cover most aspects of the lifestyle which can be anticipated in the countries concerned with particular reference to cultural differences.

Shorter courses, lasting one day, are organised by the Women's Corona Society. These courses cover family and health aspects in some detail and the Society provides detailed notes on most countries. The Corona provides more than just courses, however. There are branches of the Society in many countries and members will be introduced to a circle of expatriate women within days of arrival. The local branches are often involved in voluntary work, fund raising, and the like and the emphasis is distinctly social. In the UK, apart from organising briefing courses, the Society provides an escort service for children to see them from school to the airport. If an overnight stay is necessary the children are accommodated with Corona members. The cost is minimal and the service is, understandably, very well used.

Many companies, well versed in the ways of expatriates, do not use or recommend these courses, but rather organise their own, calling on the company's wide experience and that of existing staff.

These courses are less frequently open to wives but if at all possible the would-be expatriate wife should make clear her desire to attend.

On the financial front, too, it is important that wives are involved. From my own experience in financial counselling it is very often the wife who controls the family finances and who asks the most detailed and searching questions on tax and investment. As a rule, she is also much less likely to accept readily a sales pitch for more speculative ventures.

Many employers will also spend a great deal of money ensuring that their employees have a working knowledge of the local language before sending them abroad. Few will include wives in this but language may be of even greater importance to them. Wives will normally have to deal with tradesmen, servants and others who may have little, if any, grasp of English. Not only will a basic understanding of the local language make the wife more effective, it will also help her own self-confidence in the alien environment. An investment in a language course can be money well spent.

In many countries, but particularly in the third world and some Middle Eastern countries, the role of women and their place in society is vastly different from that in the UK and other Western countries. There may be restrictions on the way women dress, where they may go, and what activities they may indulge in. In Saudi Arabia, a woman is not allowed to drive and is not advised to go anywhere unless accompanied by her husband or other acceptable male.

Restrictions are also common where work permits are concerned. For a career-minded woman this can be a particularly difficult problem. Where both spouses have careers in the UK the disruption of the wife's career can be a source of discontent and resentment. Some employers will compensate the family financially by making an allowance for the loss of a wife's earnings but that is rarely the point at issue. However, depending on the particular career and the country the family go to, there may be some possibility of the wife continuing her work. Generally women with a medical or education background will be able to find work and secretarial work is often available even in countries which appear repressive of women. But in most other jobs where employment, rather than self-employment, is involved, there may be few opportunities.

Last, but far from being least of an expatriate wife's problems, may be her husband. The girlie bars of Wanchai may be one worry but more likely, her greatest worry will be how little time he spends with her and the family. As mentioned elsewhere in this book, most expatriates work longer hours than is common in the UK. This has a major impact on the wife, not simply because she is left alone for longer but because much more of the household responsibility devolves to her. While in some countries there may be servants to ease the drudgery of housework, looking after and supervising them may make doing it all yourself an even more appealing prospect.

The expatriate wife is a very special sort of lady if she is to be successful. Fortunately, most British women succeed and enjoy themselves immensely.

EDUCATION

When the breadwinner becomes an expatriate the whole family is affected, not least the children. Where the family goes too, the disruption can verge on chaos and one of the first casualties can be the children's education. However, this need not arise if preparations are made as far in advance as possible, the various alternatives considered and discussed, and the children themselves, if they are old enough, kept closely involved. There are three basic options for the expatriate family:

(1) teach children in the home; or
(2) send them to a school abroad; or
(3) send them to school in the UK.

Each of these options has many advantages and not a few drawbacks but the actual decision made will, of course, depend on individual circumstances. The aim of this section is simply to highlight the pros and cons of each and, perhaps, provide some guidelines for the expatriate parent. It cannot, however, take the place of a consultation with a professional education counsellor.

Teaching in the home

Where one or other parent is or has been a school teacher this option may appear eminently suitable and acceptable. Where there is no teaching experience in the family the reaction to such a suggestion is likely to be along the lines that it is impossible, parents would be unable to cope, the children would suffer. This need not be the case at all. Although home teaching is most appropriate for young children of primary school age, many expatriates have seen their children progress to 'O' and 'A' levels without the benefit of a traditional school. But this is not an easy option. It demands a major commitment from the parents, and generally most from the mother. Fortunately there are organisations which can offer a great deal of help and professional back-up to the family teachers.

For children in the 5-15 age group the Worldwide Education Service (WES) of the Parents' National Educational Union (PNEU) is the most important source of teaching materials, assistance and advice. WES caters for children educated at home in over 120 countries and provides teaching packages or tuition packs suitable for all ability levels up to GCSE standard. The curriculum is that of the PNEU schools which is widely respected. The teaching does not prepare a child for any particular examination at that level but the general standard reached is similar. In addition to dealing with individual families and children, WES will also advise on setting up small schools where there is a sufficiently large expatriate community to warrant one, such as a large construction or engineering project or oil operation. In some cases WES will provide the whole system from obtaining premises to engaging teachers.

For older children or those for whom GCSE or 'A' levels are required, home teaching will involve the more common types of correspondence courses. These are available from a number of organi-

103

sations and in some cases can be supplemented by summer schools or other short residential courses. Learning by correspondence is difficult and requires much discipline and dedication on the part of the child and a great deal of encouragement from parents if it is to be successful. The address of WES and some correspondence tutors is given in chapter 10.

Overseas schools
When home schooling is not a viable option parents are then faced with the choice of educating their children locally or back in the UK (or possibly in some third country). UK schools are discussed in the final section; this part deals with English language schools outside the UK.

In most expatriate centres these days there are usually primary level schools using the English language. In countries where English is not the main language these schools will generally have been established purely to cater for expatriate children. But that is not to say that they will cater exclusively for British children, either in intake or in curriculum. With the large numbers of American expatriates in Europe, the Middle and Far East, many schools are based on the American education system. This will not present a problem for children up to the age of ten or thereabouts but if it is intended that the children go on to private school in the UK for their secondary education then they will need preparation for the Common Entrance Examination. Few overseas schools prepare children for this, so a return to a UK prep school may be the only option at the age of ten.

Expatriate and international schools at all levels are usually fee paying and there are generally waiting lists of between a few months and a couple of years. Where a local school abroad is to be used it is essential to check the charges and waiting list beforehand and also find out what degree of assistance will be given by the expatriate employer.

Expatriate English schools are much less common at the secondary level. The traditional education of the British expatriate child is the British boarding school from age ten or eleven and despite steeply rising costs these schools continue to be the first resort of most expatriate parents. American expatriates, however, have been much more ready to establish local schools for their expatriate children and there are now many American international schools around the world. Obviously these schools are basically designed to suit children for entrance to American colleges and universities and are thus less appropriate to the needs of British children, but several of these schools now offer study for the International Baccalaureate which is rapidly becoming an internationally acceptable certificate of academic competence. The IB course of study is also offered by many other international schools and several whose main intake is of British children. Most British higher education institutions now recognise the IB Diploma as being equivalent to an 'A' level course. In many countries there are British schools whose curriculum is based on GCSE and 'A' level lines and, for the child transferred abroad in mid-course, these are obviously most suitable. Similarly, if the child's education will not be completed abroad it is necessary to consider the compatability of his overseas course with what will be available either on return to the UK or, indeed, on a transfer to another country overseas.

What secondary education means for expatriate parents, therefore, is much more long-term thinking than is necessary for younger children. Then again, there is the financial aspect; international schools are almost invariably expensive, some more so than British boarding schools. Where there is a local international school, many expatriate employers will provide assistance with fees and some will only provide fees for these schools. Most employers, however, will provide an education allowance which can be used at any school and most of this money, for the British expatriate at least, ends up in the British private education establishment.

UK schools

As mentioned earlier the traditional education for the children of British expatriates is in the UK boarding schools and this shows little sign of changing. What has changed is the type of expatriate. In years past most children at boarding school came from families for whom such an education would be taken as a matter of course. These days the private sector generally is largely populated by children whose parents did not, themselves, enjoy, if that is the correct word, a residential or private education. For the children, resilient souls that they usually are, this presents few problems, but for the parents it can be more difficult. Not least of these difficulties is in choosing a school and deciding at what age the child should be enrolled. But professional advice is available from such organisations as WES, the Independent Schools Information Service, and educational trusts such as Gabbitas-Thring and Truman & Knightly. Also there is a major reference book — *The Parents' Guide to Independent Schools* — published by SFIA Educational Trust (7th edn. £27 o'seas inc p&p).

But, before searching for a UK boarding school, the expatriate parent should consider all the other options. The overseas alternatives have been described but even these may not be necessary or even desirable. For older children coming up to GCSE or 'A' levels it might be in their best interests to stay put. If they can live with relatives or friends during term time this may be in their best interests. Alternatively, one or two state schools do have provision for some boarders who usually are the children of expatriate parents. Where local relatives are not available it might be possible for a child to be transferred to another state school and live with relatives in that locality or to transfer to a private day school if the local state school is fully subscribed.

Where the choice comes down to schools in the private sector the variety is enormous. There are some 2,400 private schools in Britain and, despite various political noises about their future abolition, most continue to thrive. There are basically two types of private schools — preparatory schools which take children in the age range 8-13, and senior schools taking pupils from 13-18 (but some girls' senior schools accept pupils from age 11). There are also many pre-prep schools taking children from age 3 upwards but boarding facilities are rarely offered below age 7. Co-education schools are becoming more popular but the majority remain single sex at least until the sixth form.

The preparatory schools, as their name implies, prepare their pupils for their senior school careers and specifically for the Common Entrance Examination, the major qualification for entry to private secondary schools. Not all prep schools do this, however, as many have their own associated senior schools, entrance to which is by internal evaluation rather than an external test. Detailed guidance on how to go about choosing a school for any child cannot be given in this book but some of the factors which might usefully be kept in mind include:

(1) Religion: many independent schools have strong religious affiliations even if they accept pupils of denominations outside their own.
(2) Academic record: the academic record and achievement of the independent sector as a whole is far superior to that of the state sector but some schools lay greater stress on this than others.
(3) Extra-curricular activities: some schools offer a wide variety of hobbies, sports, community service and other ways of passing leisure time.
(4) Special courses and assistance: some independent schools have developed a reputation in a particular sphere such as science or music and others provide special assistance to children with learning difficulties.
(5) Size of school: biggest is by no means always best, what is more important is the staff/pupil ratio and the mix of pupils and variety of courses available.
(6) Location of school: for children travelling abroad each holiday the more efficient the connecting communications are, the better; where children are to stay with relatives or friends during half term or other holidays, their proximity is also important.
(7) Fees: the cost of boarding a child at prep school is unlikely to be less than £4,500 per annum and for senior school the minimum is around £5,000 per annum. These fees have risen substantially in recent years and are likely to increase further.

The last two items above, location of school and fees, need some further discussion. Where children, particularly younger ones, have to get from school to their parents abroad it is essential that some sort of escort service is used. Most airlines are experienced in handling young travellers so the latter part of the trip is generally satisfactory but the school to airport part can be troublesome. Some schools operate their own escort service and this can be extremely valuable, not to say reassuring. If the service is not available from the school there are private agencies which can help, such as Country Cousins. Members of the Women's Corona Society can also make use of that organisation's children's escort service. Also relevant at this point is the appointment of a guardian — most schools insist on this — preferably someone reasonably accessible and who will look after

children during the short breaks if they are not to join their parents. Country Cousins and another organisation — Universal Aunts — will also undertake this latter duty.

For most expatriates, school fees are not a major consideration since assistance with these is commonly given by employers. But since fees have risen so much many employers these days provide only partial funding, commonly £2,500-£3,000 per annum per child. For a large family this can leave a substantial shortfall to be met personally. In addition the parents will usually have to meet personally the costs of uniform, extra-curricular activities, special tuition and some travel costs. On this last point, most employers will allow one or two return trips each year for children at school in the UK, any other travelling such as in the third vacation will be at the parents' expense. Since interrupting a child's education is unlikely to be to his or her benefit many parents intend to leave their children in the private sector even after their own return to the UK. Where this is the case some form of school fee planning is advisable. There are several organisations which describe themselves as school fee specialists who, in fact, specialise in insurance broking. Insurance policies can be useful for school fees but school fee planning is not some esoteric art, it is merely a function of investment and a non- insurance investment strategy can be just as efficient and will often be much more flexible. (see chapter 6)

Higher education
Finally, turning to higher education, many expatriate parents have experienced great difficulty in obtaining university or other higher education grants for their children. Similarly many children have been classified as overseas students and have had to pay the higher rate of fees. At the present time there is still some confusion about grants and fees as applied to the children of expatriates and advice should be sought from the Department of Education and Science on specific cases or from specialist education consultants.

MEDICAL CONSIDERATIONS
Medical and health considerations are important everywhere but for the expatriate and his family in the tropics, or in countries where medical facilities are less readily available than at home, these considerations are essential. Apart from any vaccinations which might be necessary for entry into a country, there are a variety of precautions and checks which most expatriates should undergo before leaving the UK. Some employers will arrange for all of these for their employees and a few will include all members of the family. But even the best company doctor will be limited in what he can provide and the individual should ensure, himself, that he has done everything that is required.

Before leaving the UK
As soon as the decision to go abroad has been made every member of the family should have a comprehensive medical check-up. In addition to the normal health check, this should include any dental

treatment which is necessary or which is imminent, eye tests should be done and any spectacles or contact lenses acquired (preferably with a spare set) before departure, a visit to a chiropodist would not go amiss and, for women, a visit to a family planning clinic if appropriate. Where any regular medication or any contraceptives are required, it may be advisable to obtain a stock of these plus detailed information and instruction from the expatriate's doctor for any doctor who may need to be consulted overseas.

Where inoculations are required these should be planned as far in advance as possible so that any adverse reactions are spotted or dealt with before leaving. Many vaccinations do not provide complete protection, some are required by the destination country although against World Health Organisation advice, and some are simply sensible precautions. Among those in the first category is the cholera vaccine which, unless mandatory or because an outbreak of the disease is probable in the country concerned, should not be given as a matter of course. Smallpox has, officially, been eradicated and vaccination should not be required anywhere. Yellow fever vaccine is necessary if the expatriate will be visiting or passing in transit through an infected area. Among the sensible vaccinations are those for typhoid and paratyphoid, polio and tetanus. Inoculations for very young children should also be considered before leaving home.

Overseas

Anti-malarial tablets are perhaps among the commonest pills taken by expatriates and it is essential that these are taken regularly wherever the disease is endemic. Most courses should be started before arrival abroad and it is essential that the doctor who prescribes should know which country is concerned since the malarial parasite in certain countries has developed resistance against the commonest drug proguanil (Paludrine). It is also necessary to continue this medication after leaving a malarial area for at least the next four weeks.

Advice for expatriates when abroad is very much common sense. Fungal infections thrive in or on damp skin, so in hot climates frequent washing and the wearing of absorbent clothing is the order of the day. The diseases of insanitation can generally be avoided by taking care in washing and cooking food and by inoculation in the case of the more serious problems such as typhoid, polio and hepatitis. Worm infections often picked up on the feet indicate the need to wear shoes always and this can be of particular relevance to children.

Insect pests and the diseases they bring can be dealt with by repellent creams, sprays, and in the case of malaria, by tablets. Bites, stings and burrowing insects and maggots are troublesome but rarely serious if the expatriate is aware of the beast responsible and he seeks medical attention immediately.

On return to the UK

In the event of illness after returning to the UK, it is essential that whoever is giving the treatment is informed of the spell spent abroad so that any tropical or other non-local types of infection can be considered.

Medical care and insurance

The intending expatriate should find out as much as possible about the medical facilities and the standard of health care he can expect at his destination. Although several countries operate a welfare health service similar to or better than the UK National Health Service, it may be available free only to local people. In many developing countries facilities of a reasonable standard may be few and far between or, as is the case in most countries around the world, whatever facilities there are, are expensive. For the great majority of expatriates this means that health insurance is essential.

Most working expatriates are provided with some degree of medical insurance by their companies but this does not always cover their families. This is a point which must be checked and, again, should be done before leaving the UK. Where cover is not provided by the employer, or the cover is insufficient, the expatriate should give high priority to obtaining cover from one or other of the UK organisations specialising in the field. The largest of these organisations is BUPA (British United Provident Association) with PPP (Private Patient's Plan) not far behind. But apart from these two there are other, smaller, organisations whose medical insurance schemes for expatriates are well worth considering. These include: Exeter Hospital Aid Society, Western Provident Association, Bristol Contributory Welfare Association, and other insured schemes available from specialist expatriate brokers.

The plans offered by these organisations vary in the amount of cover provided and the charges made. Most allow the individual to choose the amount of cover required and the two larger associations will provide advice on the cover considered most appropriate to individual countries. Generally the medical insurance schemes come with a wide range of optional extras and cost is determined by the age of the insured, but average cover for a family with two children should be available for between £400 and £600 per annum. What the expatriate should check first is the average cost of hospitalisation, as this is often the largest item on a treatment bill with some hospitals charging £200 or more each day, and choose his level of cover accordingly.

In addition to the medical insurance itself, it may be advisable to include insurance for repatriation. This is particularly where local facilities are sparse or not sufficiently sophisticated for major surgery. On its own this insurance is not cheap but it can often be included in a package with the medical insurance at a reduced rate.

Large discounts are obtainable on private medical insurance for groups of people so, if the expatriate employer does not have a scheme, it may be worthwhile suggesting it even if all contributions are paid by the staff. Failing that, some of the insurers will accept a small informal group without a common employer if one member of the group handles the administration.

DEATH OVERSEAS

Of the two certainties in life, death and taxes, the latter has been described in chapter 3. Where a person dies overseas the tragedy can be made much worse than would be the case at home. This is particularly so where the deceased's family have remained in the UK and funeral arrangements, etc, have to be made at long distance. In many countries, especially in the tropics, it is a local legal requirement that corpses are buried or cremated immediately or very shortly after death. In such cases it is vital that the expatriate's family be contacted at the very earliest opportunity. It is commonly the family's wish that the body should be returned to the UK and arrangements must be made for this either through the local employer or, on occasion, through the British Embassy. The cost of repatriating a body is substantial and any local representative will normally need to be satisfied that these costs will be met (although for employees of major companies this is unlikely to be an important factor). Certain medical insurance/repatriation packages will also cover the shipment of a corpse.

The problems of death overseas are obviously greatest where the family remain at home but even where the family are together overseas the administration can cause major difficulty. Local legal advice and assistance from the British Embassy should be sought immediately.

WILLS AND LEGAL ARRANGEMENTS

On all aspects of legal arrangements there is no substitute for proper legal advice. Most expatriate clubs have their share of bar room lawyers as well as dinner table tycoons and tax experts. The advice proffered by these worthies will encompass everything from how to do your own conveyancing to how to make a killing on the Mozambique Stock Exchange. The best advice the new expatriate can get is to ignore all of this and listen only to those who are properly qualified. Nowhere is this more important than in the preparation of a will.

Making a will is something most of us put off, and put off, and put off again. The eventual result is death in intestacy when one's property is disposed of according to the rules of intestacy rather than as the deceased might have wished. To avoid intestacy, a valid will must be made and it is important that this be drawn up with the assistance of a solicitor. Not only does a will allow for desired bequests, it can also be an instrument of tax planning, generally for the avoidance or minimisation of inheritance tax. For the expatriate, making a will is especially important since his property is likely to be more widely spread than his UK based contemporaries' and his affairs generally can be expected to be more complex.

Apart from making a will in the UK the expatriate might also consider making a second will in his country of residence. In the event of death abroad, his local assets can then be more speedily released to his beneficiaries than could be the case with a UK probate and such assets could then be used to pay any tax which falls due on the UK estate before probate can be granted. Another point the expatriate must be aware of where he has assets overseas or where he is resident, is that not all countries allow a person to dispose of his property as he wishes. It may be that a certain proportion of the estate or property

111

has to pass to a spouse or to children. Again proper legal advice must be sought at the earliest opportunity.

Other legal affairs which might concern the expatriate include drawing up a lease for letting his property. As described in the property chapter this is a complicated matter and the use of a solicitor is advisable (essential, usually, where there is a building society involved). Guardianship of children at boarding school is occasion for recourse to the family solicitor as, too, is any serious family strife. Divorce among expatriates is not noticeably higher than in any other sector of the community but it does raise additional problems.

Finally, some advisors recommend giving a solicitor power of attorney over the expatriate's UK affairs. In some cases where there are major complexities, perhaps involving property or investments, administration of the affairs of other relatives, or other dealings of a potentially urgent nature, this might be worth considering but for the majority of expatriates it is not necessary.

THE NATIONALITY ACT

The British Nationality Act 1982 was brought into force in January 1983. This Act caused a great furore during its passage through Parliament in 1981 and 1982 and it is by no means certain that it will retain its present form indefinitely. The Act set up three new types of British citizenship:

(1) *British citizenship* which was conferred automatically on 1st January 1983 on all citizens of the UK and Colonies then possessing the right of abode in the UK;
(2) *British Dependent Territories citizenship* which is conferred automatically on all citizens of the UK and Colonies deriving their status from a colony;
(3) *British overseas citizenship* which is conferred on all those citizens of the UK and Colonies who on 1st January 1983 did not automatically acquire citizenship in either of the above categories.

Of these categories, the first is of major interest to the majority of readers of this book. Now, British citizenship is available only to those with close ties to the UK and only the full British citizenship carries the right of entry to and settlement in the UK.

Another aspect of this Act is to give equal treatment to women. All women who are British citizens will be entitled to keep their citizenship on marriage to a foreigner and to pass on their citizenship to their children on the same terms as male British citizens. This provision is not retrospective, so children born to British women abroad will not automatically be British unless the father possessed the necessary citizenship qualifications.

The part of the Nationality Act of greatest interest to British expatriates concerns children born abroad and this has caused some justifiable worries in the expatriate communities. There is no immediate reason for worry in most cases but problems can arise in

112

the next generation, that is, on the citizenship of present expatriates' grandchildren. In general, a child born abroad to any British citizen will be a British citizen at birth provided one of his or her parents is British other than British by descent. Such a child will then be British by descent and, unless he qualifies under another provision of the Act, such a child will not be able automatically to pass on British citizenship to his own children. A parent who is British by descent can only pass on his citizenship on certain conditions. These are:

(1) that the parent concerned has spent three years in the UK prior to the birth and that the parent himself was born to a parent who held British citizenship other than by descent;
(2) that a child, born abroad, who accompanies his parents back to the UK and lives there continuously for three years, qualifies for registration as a British citizen as of right (this citizenship is considered as of otherwise than by descent);
(3) that children of British citizens who are serving under a European Community institution are considered British by birth regardless of where they are born; and
(4) that children of Crown Servants will also qualify for full citizenship regardless of the derivation of their parents' citizenship.

What this morass of legislation means is that the average expatriate need have no worries so long as he does not look beyond the next generation but if he does and there is no special exemption he will have to rely on the discretion of the Home Secretary who is empowered to grant British citizenship to any minor he thinks fit. This is hardly a provision on which to rely but the alternative seems to be planeloads of pregnant mothers flying home for the birth of their children.

PERSONAL SECURITY
With the ever increasing incidence of violence and the general breakdown in law and order in so many countries, expatriates are understandably becoming more concerned about their own and their families' security. As a result they may tend to demand greater assurances from their employers regarding their personal safety in the event of serious disturbances. But there is much the expatriate can do himself to reduce the risks.

Contact with the British Embassy
As a first priority new expatriates must be advised to ensure immediately on taking up their posts that they and any members of their family resident with them register their names, addresses and telephone numbers with the nearest British Embassy or Consulate. For some reason British expatriates seem reluctant to do this, certainly when compared with their American and European colleagues. It is normally the Consul who maintains contact with British nationals in periods of emergency. But registration is required not only to maintain such contact but also to enable the Embassy to estimate the numbers

involved if, as a final resort, they have to plan for an immediate evacuation.

The location of the expatriate and his degree of access to the nearest town housing an Embassy or Consulate is therefore of considerable importance and should be established by the expatriate before his departure.

Well before such a critical stage as evacuation is reached the Foreign and Commonwealth Office may wish to recommend that non-essential personnel, for example children and members of the family not actually employed, leave the country. On occasion many dependants are reluctant to take this step, preferring to stick it out together. Brave this may be, but it can also be foolish and can lead to even greater difficulties if the situation deteriorates further.

In all difficult or potentially dangerous situations a degree of liaison between the headquarters of the expatriate's company and the Foreign Office (or the State Department) is always advantageous. Then, even if the individual expatriates have not themselves registered, the company can itself inform the authorities of the personnel involved.

As a final point, an obvious but important recommendation is to listen to the BBC World Service if the local situation is worsening. There can never be any guarantee of free or uninterrupted communication between individuals and British missions in such conditions and objective news on local broadcasts may, in any event, be unlikely.

Safeguarding individuals and property

Major civil disturbances may make the headlines but much more common are personal assaults, burglary and even kidnap. In the previous section I emphasised the importance of keeping in touch with the Embassy but this must be supplemented by normal home security against break-ins, sensible precautions while on the move, and especially always knowing where the rest of the family is and how to contact them in an emergency.

Terrorist attacks, especially kidnap and personal assaults, are not easy to foresee and can be truly catastrophic in both human and financial terms. The financial cost can be hedged by insurance and premiums vary enormously with the underwriter's assessment of the risk; for example, they are much greater in Central America than in Western Europe. Because of the cost it is rare for an individual expatriate to take out such insurance himself. It is much more commonly done by companies but for obvious reasons they are reluctant to admit, even to their staff, that they have cover for kidnapping. If the expatriate, or his company, insures with the leading Lloyd's underwriters in this field their package will include advice from a visiting security consultant and, in the event of a kidnap, the provision of a consultant to assist in negotiating the release. For those not insured, the same consultants, such as Control Risks Ltd, can be engaged privately. A personal security survey in an overseas location comprises a review of the expatriate's lifestyle and that of other members of the family, the home environment and the means and route of getting to work, school, etc. in order to assess where the principal dangers lie. The consultancy fees involved tend to be about £350 per day, plus the consultant's travelling costs and the cost of any equipment and its installation if this is required. Obviously, such a procedure is not cheap, but the unit cost can be substantially reduced by combining several surveys within a company or expatriate group. A more restricted package is available for home security only. This will be tailored to the expatriate's needs as far as possible before he goes overseas and is provided for a flat, a town house or a detached residence. Obviously, to make use of this package the expatriate must have as much detail as possible from his employer about the type of housing to be provided. The package includes a further consultation by letter or telephone to discuss its application to the actual situation the expatriate finds on arrival overseas. The fee for this type of package is likely to be about £200 plus equipment.

To conclude, the responsibility for the expatriate's personal security lies with both the individual and his employer, and both can take sensible precautions to reduce the risk involved. Most importantly, people who are seen to take security precautions better than the average are very seldom picked as targets by either criminals or terrorists.

8

Returning home

Returning to the UK often involves as much of a shock as the original departure. But as with the departure, proper advance planning can make the transition much easier. The short term expatriate who has been abroad only two or three years will have little difficulty in adjusting to life at home but the long term expatriate, especially if his visits to the UK have been infrequent, may experience as much culture shock as he did on first arriving overseas. Life without servants during a November fog when the milkman is on strike may be enough to send the returned expatriate in search of the next plane out again.

RE-ENTERING THE SYSTEM
One of the "joys" of returning to the UK is to be greeted with an avalanche of official paperwork. It matters not that you are returning to retire, to continue working or even to join the dole queue, the multifarious government agencies all have their forms to be completed.

The 65 year-old retired expatriate (or 60 year-old in the case of female expatriates) who has not already heard from the DHSS should contact his or her local office regarding State Pension entitlements. Any expatriate returning to unemployment should also contact the local DHSS but except in the case of very short term expatriates it is unlikely that he or she will qualify for unemployment benefit. In certain circumstances other benefits may be payable depending on the individual's own resources. The returning expatriate who goes directly into employment, either with the same employer or a new one, will be contacted directly by the DHSS and the Inland Revenue. Where self-employment is involved, then the returned expatriate should again contact the DHSS to ensure continuity of National Insurance contributions. For all expatriates it will be necessary to re-register under the National Health Service with an appropriate GP.

Aspects of pre-return tax planning are covered in the next section but once the expatriate is back in the UK it is usually in his best interest to contact the Revenue at a fairly early stage. For those in employment the Revenue will themselves be in fairly rapid contact with the employee in order to calculate the appropriate tax code to be applied against the employee's salary. For those not in receipt of earnings or pension the Revenue are unlikely to be aware of their situation until they are informed directly. Various forms will have to be completed including Form P86 (which asks for information relating to the last few years, nationality, intentions of residence, etc) and a tax return for the

116

current year. Where the expatriate has acquired substantial assets over perhaps a lengthy period abroad it can often be sensible to prepare a schedule of assets for inclusion with the tax return although this particular information may not be directly requested. The rationale behind this is simply to avoid unnecessary questions and correspondence with the Inland Revenue at a later date when, perhaps, the sale of any particular asset may be reflected in increasing income under some other category in a subsequent tax return. It is essential, however, that if the expatriate is to have his tax affairs put on a sound footing from the beginning that he makes use of a professional advisor — accountant or tax specialist. The cost involved should not be great and should at least lay a solid foundation for future negotiations with the Revenue.

TAXATION

Terminating the overseas employment or simply visiting the UK will not, of themselves, change an expatriate's status from non-resident to resident. This change will only occur if the expatriate does one of the following things:

(1) he returns to the UK with the intention of remaining either permanently or for a number of years; or
(2) he spends 183 days or more in any tax year in the UK; or
(3) he visits the UK year after year for periods which average 90 or more days each year over four consecutive tax years; or
(4) he sets foot in the UK, no matter how briefly, while not in full-time employment abroad and when he has accommodation available for his use in the UK.

A person who returns to the UK between separate overseas employments may become resident for a year under the second or fourth category above but remain not ordinarily resident. This situation of resident but not ordinarily resident has its own peculiar tax consequences. Even if the period actually spent in the UK in the tax year is small, any capital gains made at any time in that tax year will be liable or potentially liable to capital gains tax. Also, all income from overseas, either earnings or investment income, so far as it is brought into the UK, will be liable to UK income tax (where tax has already been charged abroad, relief for double taxation will be granted). All income arising in the UK will also be assessable. In some respects this treatment of the short-term resident is harsher than that of the new permanent resident. It certainly means that the short-term resident has to plan his finances with a great deal of care.

On assuming or re-assuming permanent or semi-permanent UK residence the tax consequences are not necessarily any less complex but there are some useful mitigating ploys. In such a case the returning expatriate will be treated as resident and ordinarily resident from the date of his return regardless of when during the tax year this return occurs. From the date he resumes residence his worldwide income becomes liable to UK tax. At the same time, he becomes

117

entitled to full personal allowances even if he is resident for only part of the year. The result of this latter point is to give most returning expatriates a period of tax holiday after their arrival, particularly if they commence employment where they are taxed under PAYE.

The treatment of income

In the tax year of return different types of income are treated in different ways. Of greatest importance to British expatriates is the treatment of income in the following categories.

Overseas earnings

Unlike the temporary resident mentioned earlier, the new permanent resident will not have any tax liability on any earnings made from his overseas employment, whether brought back to the UK or not. This also applies to any terminal leave payments, gratuities or bonuses relating to the overseas work but paid later when the expatriate has resumed UK residence. Any lump sum payment made from a provident fund or any sum in commutation of pension rights will likewise be exempt. Any pension derived from an overseas pension fund and relating to a period of overseas work will be taxable to the extent of 90 per cent, i.e. there is 10 per cent exemption.

Overseas investment income

This becomes immediately chargeable on return to the UK and, in the case of income which is from an established source, that is, one which commenced three or more years previously, the basis of assessment is the previous year basis. This means that for a person who returns to the UK in January 1988 the income taxable is that which arose in the tax year 1986/87. By concession, the Inland Revenue will tax only a proportion of this income, the proportion being related to the amount of the tax year actually spent as a resident in the UK in the year of assessment. In the instance above, the Revenue would tax one quarter of the total since the expatriate is resident for only three months of the tax year. But even this tax can be avoided in most cases.

Income from a source which ceases prior to return escapes tax altogether so any investments sold prior to return, even if repurchased afterwards in a 'bed and breakfast' deal (see below) will not give rise to any tax liability. Similarly interest on an overseas bank deposit account can escape tax if the account is closed prior to the expatriate's return. It used to be the case that a "capitalisation" of the account would suffice for this purpose. A capitalisation simply involved a technical closure of the account but for all practical purposes the account continued. The Inland Revenue have indicated that this is considered a wholly artificial transaction and in order that the interest escape taxation the account must be physically closed and the funds transferred. For most returning expatriates this does not present a problem as it will probably be to their advantage to bring the funds onshore for deposit in, for example, a building society or, if they have no other source of taxable income, in a National Savings Bank Investment Account. With a building society account the net interest payable is fractionally higher than the gross interest available from an offshore

118

bank account, less the tax which would be payable on this. The National Savings Investment Account pays a highly competitive rate of interest and unlike other banks and building societies this is paid gross. Where the investor does want to hold his deposits offshore he can simply transfer from one bank to another or possibly even from the Jersey branch, say, to an Isle of Man branch within the same bank. However, it is still open to the Inland Revenue to challenge this as action taken purely for the purposes of avoiding tax and to be on the safe side I would recommend that the funds are relocated, if only temporarily, to the UK.

UK investment income
Most UK source income will have been taxable throughout the expatriate's stay abroad but that from exempt gilts and UK bank deposits will have been tax free. On return, the interest from gilts will become immediately taxable so, if possible, the expatriate should attempt to arrive home shortly after, rather than shortly before, an interest payment falls due. UK bank deposit interest for UK residents is now paid net of tax. What this means for the returning expatriate is that any gross payment he has received during the tax year in which he returns, albeit before his return, becomes taxable. Closing the account immediately before return does not work to save tax as it does in the case of offshore deposits. If the expatriate does hold substantial sums on deposit in the UK, it is important that these deposit accounts are closed in the tax year preceding his year of return. In this case funds could be held offshore and that account closed immediately prior to return. Now that building societies are able to pay gross interest to non-residents the same procedure should be adopted with building society deposit accounts as with UK bank deposits.

In general terms there is rarely a good reason for holding liquidity in the UK when similar returns are available from the overseas subsidiaries of British banks and where pre-return tax planning can be made much simpler.

Capital gains tax
Any capital gains realised in the tax year prior to the year of return will escape UK liability. Gains made during the year of return will be taxable whether made before or after return where the expatriate has not been not resident for 36 months prior to his return. If he has been not resident for 36 months then any gains made before return, even the day before, will escape liability. Simplistically, therefore, the expatriate should aim to realise his gains before his return but hold any assets showing losses until after his return, when such losses after realisation may be carried forward to offset future gains. However, this must be considered in conjunction with the income tax situation described earlier and, unfortunately, there is no shortcut but to do the arithmetic concerned.

Where the expatriate wishes to retain his portfolio he may crystallise some of his gains before return by a "bed and breakfast" operation. Effectively this means selling his securities one day and repurchasing them the next when, hopefully, there has been no significant price movement. The costs involved in such a transaction are not insignificant but where substantial gains are involved it may be a price well worth paying. Anyone with substantial gains should, therefore, once again take professional advice and assistance.

It is also possible for married expatriates, where one spouse is resident and the other is non resident throughout the tax year concerned, to obtain an additional benefit. The non-resident spouse may transfer to the resident spouse assets showing gains and this transaction will be treated as being carried out at market value (whether or not any cash changed hands). The base cost for any subsequent disposal would then be the market value on the date of the original transfer to the resident spouse. Such a scheme can be of particular use where properties are concerned although it must be noted that a proper conveyance would be necessary for such a scheme to be effective and this will involve, perhaps, stamp duty as well as the legal charges.

Finally, as has been mentioned elsewhere in this book, the Inland Revenue have wide powers to ignore wholly artificial transactions designed simply to secure a tax advantage. The above procedures could be prey to Revenue attack but so far they seem to have escaped.

Inheritance tax
An expatriate's liability or potential liability for inheritance tax will rarely have been altered by his change of residence. Prior to the metamorphosis of capital transfer tax into inheritance tax, shelters against liability were available both offshore and onshore. Few of these have survived the change in the law and so far no conveniently packaged inheritance tax avoidance plan has materialised (see chapter 3).

Flow charts
The flow charts on pages 121-122 give a diagramatic summary of the returning expatriate's liability to income tax and how he should go about sorting out any capital gains tax aspects. The income tax chart must be considered as a guide only, since there are many more variables in this sphere than can be encompassed in such a summary. Readers are referred back to chapter 3 — **Taxation** for more detailed advice.

INVESTMENT REVIEW
Much of an expatriate's investment review before returning will concern taxation aspects. Investments which were attractive with a tax free yield may be less useful in the UK tax environment, especially if the returning expatriate is likely to pay tax at higher rates. For these expatriates some form of tax shelter is advisable and preparations for this should be put in hand as early as possible. Among the most useful tax shelters for the returning expatriate have been the schemes offered by the insurance companies, both offshore and UK based. Much of this advantage was lost in November 1983 and in March 1984, but in certain circumstances they can still merit some attention. Of particular interest may be the possibility of placing an investment portfolio into a personalised bond fund.

Income tax

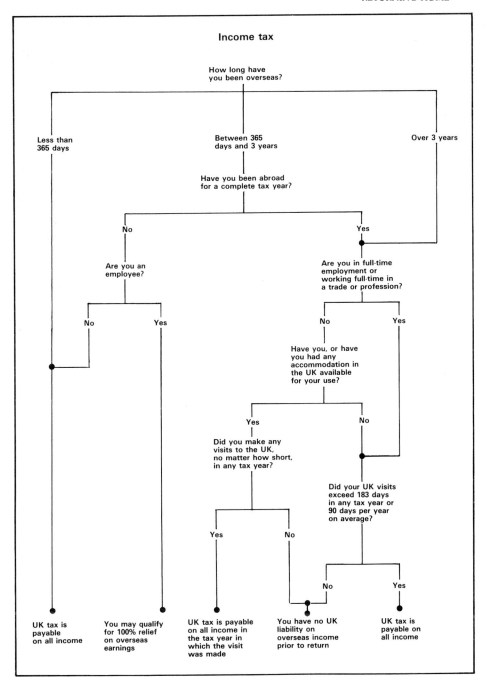

How long have you been overseas?

- Less than 365 days
- Between 365 days and 3 years
- Over 3 years

Have you been abroad for a complete tax year?

- No — **Are you an employee?**
  - No
  - Yes
- Yes — **Are you in full-time employment or working full-time in a trade or profession?**
  - No — **Have you, or have you had any accommodation in the UK available for your use?**
    - Yes — **Did you make any visits to the UK, no matter how short, in any tax year?**
      - Yes
      - No
    - No — **Did your UK visits exceed 183 days in any tax year or 90 days per year on average?**
      - No
      - Yes
  - Yes

Outcomes:
- UK tax is payable on all income
- You may qualify for 100% relief on overseas earnings
- UK tax is payable on all income in the tax year in which the visit was made
- You have no UK liability on overseas income prior to return
- UK tax is payable on all income

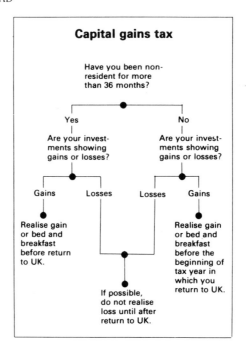

Capital gains tax

Have you been non-resident for more than 36 months?

Yes — Are your investments showing gains or losses?

No — Are your investments showing gains or losses?

Gains — Realise gain or bed and breakfast before return to UK.

Losses

Losses

Gains — Realise gain or bed and breakfast before the beginning of tax year in which you return to UK.

If possible, do not realise loss until after return to UK.

Basically this means that the investor retains personal control over his investments but by placing them within an insurance policy can put an 'insulating layer' between them and his personal tax liability. This may not preclude any charge to tax but for the wealthier investor it can certainly reduce the burden. Another possible tax shelter can be constructed through the use of offshore trusts but these are highly technical and should only be considered with the benefit of expert advice much beyond the scope of this book.

Finally, some investments not only will attract direct taxes in due course in the UK but may, on return, attract indirect tax. Care should be taken with the so-called 'alternative investments' whether they are carpets, works of art, porcelain, or whatever, and check on any duty which might be charged on import to the UK. Similarly, gold bullion coins such as kruggerands will be liable to VAT on being brought into the UK. One alternative to these duties and taxes is to have the items deposited in the Channel Islands or other offshore location.

OTHER ASPECTS

Money isn't everything and among the million and one things the returning expatriate has to consider it may not receive the priority required. Apart from problems associated with moving anywhere, notifying all and sundry of a change of address, selling the cat and the car, and arranging a farewell party, the potential repatriate should remember one thing: if he hasn't used a good advisor in the past, he probably needs one now.

122

9

Doing your homework

This book was never intended to provide any detailed guidance on the living and working conditions in the many countries frequented by British expatriates. Such an exercise would be futile in any event as the time spent gathering and assimilating such information would be such that inevitably it would be out of date by the time the book was printed. However, some general comments on a regional basis may be useful and these are provided later.

It cannot be stressed enough that advance information on any new country will make life easier and perhaps more interesting for the whole family. Several sources of information are available and you are strongly recommended to follow them up. The most important ones are as follows:

(1) The embassy or High Commission in the UK of the country to which you are going should be able to provide you with a variety of up-to-date information on many aspects of life and work there. Of particular use might be details of tax, social security, and other legal/governmental data which is likely to be completely objective. Other information may be slightly less objective or, in some cases, pure propaganda but useful nonetheless.

(2) The British Embassy or High Commission in your new country may also produce worthwhile information although this is often restricted to primarily business-oriented data. The British Overseas Trade Board likewise produces such information in a series of booklets "Hints to Exporters" which can be useful in some cases. Finally, the British Council may be able to provide some background on local culture, education, etc.

(3) Many of the British and international banks also produce guides and information sheets on many countries. The booklets provided by the Hongkong and Shanghai Bank are perhaps among the best, but as with British Embassy material, the bulk of the information is aimed at commercial and business interests. That said, the general information is highly readable and reasonably comprehensive.

(4) Most major libraries and large bookshops will offer much in the way of background reading for many expatriate locations but most commonly Europe, North America, the Caribbean and Australasia. It may be more difficult to find out about life in North Yemen or Tuvalu.

(5)   Of particular usefulness is a regularly updated range of "Expatriate Briefings" published by Monitor Press in association with the Centre for International Briefing (Farnham Castle) and The Royal Commonwealth Society. These cost £10 per country (£12 overseas) and provide a condensed but comprehensive guide under the following headings:
Overview and Background
Rules and Regulations
Living Conditions
Working Conditions
Finance and Money Matters
Family and Domestic
Education
Health and Insurance
Transport and Communications
Culture and Society
Leisure and Sport
Basic Facts and Sources of Further Information
       As with all published material some of the information goes out of date rapidly but these guides remain good value and represent perhaps the minimum homework the expatriate needs to do.
(6)   Briefing courses: mention has already been made of the briefings offered by the Centre for International Briefing and the Womens' Corona Society. The CIB briefings at Farnham Castle last for four days and provide a wealth of information and the opportunity to meet recently returned expatriates and experts on the countries concerned. Courses are organised on a regional basis but the degree of specificity available is illustrated by an anecdote about a recent Asia course. A doctor going to a particular Pacific island wanted to know what operations were common there in order to know the equipment she would need to take. The answer was provided.
       The Womens' Corona Society courses are shorter, lasting only one day, and are targeted specifically at the interests of female expatriates. But having sat in on one of these courses I can report that the areas covered are impressive and again there is usually the opportunity to talk directly with people with recent experience of the countries concerned.
       In both cases the Centre for International Briefing and Womens' Corona Society course notes and guides provide excellent reference material.

Regional notes

Europe
With continental holidays more the rule than the exception these days many intending expatriates look upon a European posting as not vastly different from a move from Aberdeen to London, say (in the latter case there might even be more culture shock involved). However, two weeks of Bacardi and sunshine on the Costa Brava is hardly

sufficient background for life as a computer programmer in Madrid.

Expatriates working in EEC countries will experience few difficulties in terms of work and residence permits and so forth. There are, however, other areas of potential difficulty. Unlike in many other parts of the world where English is the common business language, in Western Europe this is less likely. There are, of course, regional variations with English being widely spoken in Scandanavia, Holland and Germany, but much less so in France, Italy, Spain, Portugal and Greece (outside the main resort areas). While a knowledge of the local language is useful in any country, in Europe it should be considered essential.

International English-speaking schools are fairly widespread throughout the major cities of Western Europe but they can be expensive and in many cases have lengthy waiting lists. Where the overseas posting is likely to be of lengthy duration education in local schools can often be recommended, especially for younger children, whose ability to pick up a second language is often considerably greater than their parents'. Healthcare is generally of as high a standard (and in some cases higher) as in the UK but it is rarely free, at least initially. Repayment of sums spent on healthcare may be made on submitting a claim in due course. Practice does vary from country to country and the precise procedures should be established at an early opportunity.

The European countries all operate sophisticated, not to mention complicated, systems of taxation and social security. As in the UK, there is no substitute for good local advice. Employers may often help with this initially but failing that, using one of the international firms of accountants with local offices overseas should ensure that you keep on the right side of the fiscal authorities.

Expatriate work in Eastern Europe is fairly uncommon although there are several projects involving British companies and staff. It is assumed in these circumstances that the employers will provide very detailed background briefings for their employees and, in most instances, expatriate life revolves very much around the small expat community.

North America

Obviously the United States and Canada have many similarities with the UK and Western Europe. But the expatriate should be cautious about assuming he will experience no culture shock on moving to these countries. Such culture shock is often greater in those countries which superficially have greatest similarity to ourselves. The major difficulty with the US and Canada is obtaining work permits and visas in the first instance. However, if you have been offered employment there it can be assumed that your employer has sorted these aspects out on your behalf.

Obviously in such vast countries there are enormous regional variations but, in the main, British expatriates seem to adapt to life whether in Silicon Valley in California, the high pressure city life of Manhattan, or the wilderness of Alaska with remarkable ease. Living standards are generally considered higher in North America than in the UK and living costs too can be greater, although in many areas they are similar

125

to UK prices. One of the major areas of difference lies in the health service. North American healthcare is notoriously expensive and it is essential that any expatriate working in the US or Canada has adequate health cover. The UK health insurance companies can provide cover for North America but it is generally more economic to use the North American schemes for this. The education system is substantially different from that in the UK and while for younger children the local schools are perfectly adequate, for those who are likely to return to the UK system for GCSE and 'A' levels the American high school regime is less appropriate. Unless the children are expected to stay within the North American system to university level it may be advisable for them to be educated in the UK.

So far as taxation is concerned the American system is effectively "self-assessment" and while this may appear a daunting prospect, local assistance is readily available at very reasonable cost. Around tax return time you will find many accountants and taxation companies advertising their services and even setting up booths in shopping malls, etc. If your affairs are relatively uncomplicated the services of these agencies will be perfectly adequate, fast and cheap.

Middle East
With this region we get into much less familiar territory for most Britons and here it is important to have some understanding of the people, their culture, religion and history. The Arab countries, which are often seen in the West as constantly feuding among themselves or internally, share a heritage and nationalism at least as strong as any regional grouping anywhere in the world. The individual countries vary enormously and there is scope here only for the widest generalisations.

In the two previously described continents there are obvious climatic differences both within the regions and from the UK. However, the difference is much more marked in the Middle East. Arriving at Seeb Airport in Oman in July to find a temperature of 120°F with 95 per cent humidity is not a pleasant experience. On the other hand, arriving in Dubai in February to a pleasant 80°F after leaving a miserable cold, drizzly day in London can be a real pleasure. The Middle East is hot and it is essential that you come prepared. But it is important also to remember that many Middle Eastern cities, particularly those far from the coast, do experience extremes of climate and at night in winter it can become very cold indeed.

Leaving aside the climate, what sets the Middle East apart from the Western World are manners and customs largely dictated by the religion of Islam (note not Muhammadanism or any other description, likewise followers of Islam are muslims not Muhammadans). It is not suggested that every intending expatriate going to the Middle East should read the Qur'an (albeit interesting if you can find a translation), but some general background on Islam would be useful. The impact of Islam on the life of the individual countries varies significantly. In Saudi Arabia, guardian of the holy cities of Makkah and Medina, the impact is greatest and expatriates must exercise discretion and take care not to break the rules. Alcohol is forbidden in Saudi

Arabia and while "flash" sediki and other home brews are widely produced, they are not condoned by the authorities and condign punishment awaits any expatriate found with an illicit still. Likewise, all pork products are strictly forbidden and your longing for a good English banger or traditional British breakfast must await your next leave. The position of women in Saudi Arabia is also more difficult than in most other Gulf states and they must be careful to dress appropriately when outside the home — covering limbs and preferably wearing a black robe. Women should not venture out alone but only in the company of their husbands or another acceptable male. Note, too, that women are not allowed to drive in Saudi Arabia.

The strictures of Islam are applied less rigorously in other Gulf states with liquor being freely available in Bahrain, Dubai, Oman and certain other countries in hotels (and on occasion even in pubs). Other countries allow expatriates (non-Muslim) a liquor quota for home consumption.

Arabs of whatever walk of life are almost always exceedingly polite. Protocol is of the greatest importance. Business dealings with Arabs can prove frustrating to new expatriates as the person you are dealing with may be conducting discussions with several different people in the same room at the same time, there is much small talk and there can be endless cups of tea and coffee. In many cases this way of doing business is changing but the watchword for any expatriate in the Middle East is patience.

During Ramadan — the month of fasting — Arabs neither eat, drink, nor smoke between sunrise and sunset. During this period expatriates are strongly requested not to do any of these themselves in public.

Turning to other aspects of expatriate life the Middle East offers many opportunities and advantages. Sports facilities and all outdoor facilities are generally excellent and in most areas expatriates enjoy a very good social life. Most cities have international schools on either the English or American curriculum; healthcare in many countries is excellent (and often free) and personal taxation is either minimal or non-existent.

In Islamic countries Friday is the weekly holiday with the weekend normally starting on Thursday afternoon although the two day weekend (Thursday/Friday) is becoming more common. Business hours vary according to the nature of employment but work normally starts very early by UK standards but may finish equally early or with a lengthy midday rest period (commonly 12.00 - 3.00) and continuing till 5.00 or 6.00 in the evening.

Few expatriates return from a spell in the Middle East without a collection of "souvenirs" — be they brass camels, coffee pots, Persian rugs or some incredibly ornate jewellery. The traditional souk shopping still exists but modern souks owe more to the American idea of shopping malls than the traditional open market. That said, haggling over price remains *de rigueur* even in the main stores. "Discount" is almost always available if you insist. One point to note about shopping in Saudi Arabia is that during each prayer time the shops are closed and you will be asked to leave even if you are in the middle of a transaction for the 15 minutes or so of prayer.

The Far East

As with the Middle East perhaps the first thing which will strike the new expatriate on arrival, whether in Hong Kong, Manila or Singapore, is the enormous difference in climate. But unlike the Middle East, where arrival in a downpour of rain is possible albeit uncommon, the tropical welcome in the Far East may well be very wet indeed.

The region variously described as the Orient or the Far East contains a massive diversity of countries, life styles, cultures and expatriate opportunities. But common to most countries and certainly those of interest to most British expatriates is an overwhelming sense of people. Causeway Bay and Wanchai in Hong Kong at 2.00 in the morning bear more resemblance to London's Oxford Street at midday on Saturday than anything else. In oriental cities crowds of people are everywhere. This can lead to fairly intense feelings of claustrophobia in some places although even in the most populous cities there are areas of some tranquillity. With one or two exceptions the next impression after ''people power'' is of almost frenetic activity and industriousness. The expatriate who goes to the Far East must expect to work hard and to play hard.

The overcrowding of most of the Far Eastern cities puts accommodation at a premium and, unless this is met by the expatriate's employer, is likely to be the largest item on his or her budget. In some cases recently the cost to the employer of the expatriate's accommodation has been several times the level of the employee's salary. In other respects living in the Far East can be very economical. In fact, it has been said that you could go bankrupt saving money in Hong Kong and Singapore since so many consumer items are that much cheaper than in the UK. For the city dwelling expatriate in most Far Eastern countries life can be a gay social whirl both within the expatriate community and in the varied night life available. Even Kuala Lumpur, which has been described as ''indescribably boring'' has its moments.

The up-country expatriate, however, may find life vastly different. Few Far Eastern countries, with some obvious exceptions such as Hong Kong, Singapore and Japan, have a highly developed infrastructure. To western eyes much of the rural orient is at a very primitive level of development. However with continuing economic success in most countries this is changing and the best (and the worst) of 20th century development is rapidly encroaching.

Healthcare in tropical countries is of vital importance. The standard of care in many Far Eastern countries is extremely good but rarely free, and proper insurance is essential. Innoculation and proper medication is essential and any intending oriental expatriate should ensure that he or she is properly briefed on the health situation of whichever country he or she is visiting. Once abroad, commonsense precautions will avoid much potential harm — do not walk around barefoot in the garden, warn children not to stick their fingers into holes in the ground, shake out footwear, etc, before using and if you see a snake do not scream and run away but give the beast a chance to go quietly as most of them will.

128

So far as education is concerned there is again a major divergence between those based in the cities and those in the hinterland. Most Far Eastern cities have international schools, but with the exception of Hong Kong and Singapore these are predominantly American oriented. For expatriates based outside the cities UK education is most likely to be the answer at all levels.

Culturally there is great divergence among the multitude of countries in the area. Generally speaking, however, the correct protocol and politeness is most important. The role of women in many oriental societies remains restricted but this is changing and, not unnaturally, the change is most rapid in urban areas. Finally, a word about China — potentially one of the greatest employers of expatriates. At the present time expatriate employment in China is at a relatively low level and the restrictions placed on overseas visitors are not dissimilar to those in Eastern Europe. Over the next decade or thereabouts there are likely to be significant opportunities for British and other expatriates and their employers in the Chinese mainland and perhaps this will mop up the pool of "surplus" expatriates coming from the Middle East. In the meantime, anyone expecting to work in China should expect to be fully briefed by his employer beforehand.

Africa

Perhaps one of the most important things to remember about going to work on the African continent is that, with few exceptions, the African states are very "new". The "wind of change" of the early 50's affected not only the British Empire but the empires of the other European powers and independence of the various countries concerned largely stems from that time. In addition to being "young countries" most African states are also poor and some of them totally bankrupt, depending almost entirely on aid from international agencies and particular countries. It is probably true that most expatriates outside South Africa, Kenya and, to an extent, Nigeria, are working on projects funded by such organisations as the United Nations, the World Bank, the World Health Organisation, etc. However, the apparent poverty in most of these countries is not necessarily reflected in the expatriate lifestyle and living conditions.

The main areas of concern for most expatriates in most of Africa involve health, political stability and personal security, education and finance. Proper healthcare briefings are essential and sensible precautions regarding hygiene, appropriate clothing and some slight curbing of children's curiosity, will go a long way to protecting the expatriate family from major disaster. On the question of personal security and political instability please see chapter 7.

Educational standards vary from country to country and some have first class international or English schools but the majority do not. Where there is a substantial community of British expatriates there may be a community run school such as those provided by the Worldwide Education Service (again see chapter 7).

As with the Far East described earlier, there is a major difference in the quality of life and the facilities available to expatriates living in the quality of life and the facilities available to expatriates living in cities compared to those living up-country. However, regardless of where the expatriate lives he may well encounter problems on the financial front. This is likely to be primarily concerned with exchange controls where he is paid locally. Most African countries operate strict control and expatriation of funds can prove extremely difficult. For this reason, any expatriate working in Africa must ensure that either he will be able to repatriate his funds or that he will be paid outside his country of residence. Personal taxation also varies widely from country to country and should be investigated well in advance.

Several African countries are Islamic or have a large muslim population. In such countries the strictures of the religion are perhaps less rigorous than in certain middle eastern states but due consideration should be given to such obvious points as alcohol consumption, the position and dress of women and the particular rigours of Ramadan.

The main exceptions to what has gone before are South Africa and to a degree Kenya. In many respects for white expatriates South Africa has certain similarities with Western Europe and North America. However, the political structure and unrest does make an enormous difference. The degree to which South Africa's apartheid policy will impinge on the expatriate's lifestyle will be very much an individual consideration and while for some this may be very minor, for others it renders the country untenable. Kenya has long been a favoured destination for many British expatriates and has much to offer. Nonetheless, it does suffer from many of the common problems of other black African states although generally to a lesser extent.

Climatically Africa offers variety from tropical jungle to arid desert and generalisations are unhelpful. Country-specific information must be sought before departure.

Worldwide

The above comments on the various regions of the world come largely from personal experience of visiting expatriates in those countries and discussing with them the problems and pleasures they have found in their postings. I would finish the main text of this book with two further thoughts — as mentioned in the preface expatriates tend to be a hardy and independent breed. They need to be because in nine countries out of ten they will be very much on their own, and any two people asked for advice will invariably give contradictory answers. Secondly, they will find that as expatriates they work much harder than would be the norm in the UK, whether or not it is the six day week of Islamic countries or a five day week working from 8.00 am to 8.00 pm. But the rewards, both material and spiritual, can make it all worthwhile.

Further information

Throughout this book various organisations, government departments, and publications have been referred to. The names and addresses of all of these are produced below under the chapter in which they are mentioned.

Chapter 1 Introduction
The Centre for International
  Briefing
The Castle
Farnham
Surrey GU9 0AG

The Women's Corona Society
Room E501
Eland House
Stag Lane
London SW1E 5DH

Chapter 2 Getting a job abroad
Resident Abroad
Editorial:
The Financial Times Business
  Information Limited
102 Clerkenwell Road
London EC1M 5SA

Subscriptions:
The Financial Times Business
  Information Limited
Greystoke Place
Fetter Lane
London EC4A 1ND

PER Overseas
4-5 Grosvenor Place
London SW1X 7SB

British Association of Removers
279 Grays Inn Road
London SW1X 8SY

Women's Corona Society — see
  under chapter 1 above.

Chapter 3 Taxation
For Revenue leaflets, double
  taxation agreements, etc:
The Secretary
The Board of Inland Revenue
Somerset House
The Strand
London WC2R 1LB

Inspector of Foreign Dividends
Lynwood Road
Thames Ditton
Surrey KT7 0DP

Claims Branch (Foreign
  Division)
Magdalene House
Trinity Road
Bootle
Lancashire L69 9BB

Chapter 4 National Insurance
Department of Health and
  Social Security
Overseas Branch
Newcastle upon Tyne
NE98 1YX

**Chapter 5 Investment and
  financial planning**
Money Management
Financial Times Business
  Information Limited
Greystoke Place
Fetter Lane
London EC4A 1ND

Resident Abroad — see under
chapter 2 above

*The Unit Trust Year Book,
  The Expatriate's Guide to
  Savings and Investment,
  The Offshore Fund Year Book*
Financial Times Business
  Information Limited
7th Floor, 50-64 Broadway
London SW1H 0DB

Money International
Sweeney Bourke McAllister Ltd
Thames House
18 Park Street
London SE1 9ER

Investment International
Financial Magazines Ltd
Boundary House
91-93 Charterhouse Street
London EC1M 6NR

Middle East Expatriate
Al Hilal Publishing
PO Box 224
Manama
Bahrain

Far East Expatriate
Al Hilal Publishing (Far East)
  Pte Ltd
21st Floor
Washington Plaza
230 Wanchai Road
Hong Kong

The Expatriate
Expatriate Publications Ltd
25 Brighton Road
South Croydon
CR2 6EA

Chapter 7 Family matters
The Women's Corona Society —
  see under chapter 1 above.

The Centre for International
  Briefing — see under chapter
  1 above.

Worldwide Educational Service
Murray House
Vandon Street
London SW1H 0AJ

British Council
Central Information Service
10 Spring Gardens
London SW1A 2BN

European Council of
  International Schools
18 Lavant Street
Petersfield
Hampshire GU32 3EW

Independent Schools
  Information Service
26 Caxton Street
London SW1H 0RG

Gabbitas-Thring
6 Sackville Street
London W1X 2BR

Truman & Knightley
76-78 Notting Hill Gate
London W11 3LJ

SFIA Educational Trust
10 Queen Street
Maidenhead
Berkshire

Country Cousins
6 Springfield Road
Horsham
West Sussex RH12 2PB

Universal Aunts
36 Walpole Street
Chelsea
London SW3

Mercer's College
  (Correspondence)
Ware
Hertfordshire

Wolsey Hall (Correspondence)
Oxford OX2 6PR

BUPA International
Equity and Law House
102 Queen's Road
Brighton
Sussex BN1 3XT

PPP
Eynsham House
Tunbridge Wells
Kent TN1 2PL

Exeter Hospital Aid Society
5&7 Palace Gate
Exeter EX1 1UE

Bristol Contributory Welfare
  Association
Bristol House
40/56 Victoria Street
Bristol BS1 6AB

Western Provident Association
Culverhouse
Culver Street
Bristol BS1 5JE

Chapter 9 Guide to main expatriate centres

Employment Conditions Abroad
  Limited
Anchor House
15-19 Britten Street
London SW3 3TY

Royal Commonwealth Society
Northumberland Avenue
London WC2N 5BJ

The Centre for International
  Briefing — see under chapter
  1 above.

The Women's Corona Society —
  see under chapter 1 above.

Monitor Press
Rectory Road
Great Waldingfield
Sudbury
Suffolk CO10 0TL

Appendixes

APPENDIX 1   UK TAX RATES AND ALLOWANCES 1987/88

Income Tax:

Tax Rates

Taxable income	Rate
£	%
1 - 17,900	27
17,901 - 20,400	40
20,401 - 25,400	45
25,401 - 33,300	50
33,301 - 41,200	55
over 41,200	60

Personal allowances

Single/wife's earnings	£2,425
Married	£3,795
Additional personal/ Widow's bereavement	£1,370
Age allowance:	
65 or over : single	£2,960
: married	£4,675
80 or over : single	£3,070
: married	£4,845

(reduced by 2/3 for income over £9,800)

Capital Gains Tax:

Rate	30%
Exemption:	
individuals	£6,600
trustees	£3,300

Inheritance Tax:

Full Rate

Cumulative chargeable transfers (gross)	Rate
£	%
1 - 90,000	0
90,001 - 140,000	30
140,001 - 220,000	40
220,001 - 330,000	50
over 330,000	60

Lifetime chargeable transfers are taxed at 50% of full rate

Tapering relief (death within 7 years of transfer/gift)

Years between gift and death	% of full rate charged
0 - 3	100
3 - 4	80
4 - 5	60
5 - 6	40
6 - 7	20

APPENDIX II
Extracts from the text of the 1977 OECD Model Agreement (double taxation).

Article 1 Personal scope
This convention shall apply to persons who are residents of one or both of the Contracting States.

Article 2 Taxes covered
(1) This Convention shall apply to taxes on income and on capital imposed on behalf of a Contracting State or of its political subdivisions or local authorities, irrespective of the manner in which they are levied.

Article 4 Resident
(1) For the purposes of this Convention, the term "resident of a Contracting State" means any person who, under the laws of that State, is liable to tax therein by reason of his domicile, residence, place of management or any other criterion of a similar nature. But this term does not include any person who is liable to tax in that State in respect only of income from sources in that State or capital situated there in.
(2) Where by reason of the provisions of paragraph 1 an individual is a resident of both Contracting States, then his status shall be determined as follows:
  (a) he shall be deemed to be a resident of the State in which he has a permanent home available to him; if he has a permanent home available to him in both States, he shall be deemed to be a resident of the State with which his personal and economic relations are closer (centre of vital interests);
  (b) if the State in which he has his centre of vital interests cannot be determined, or if he has not a permanent home available to him in either State, he shall be deemed to be a resident of the State in which he has an habitual abode;
  (c) if he has an habitual abode in both States or in neither of them, he shall be deemed to be a resident of the State of which he is a national;

135

(d) if he is a national of both States or of neither of them, the competent authorities of the Contracting States shall settle the question by mutual agreement.

(3) Where by reason of the provisions of paragraph 1 a person other than an individual is a resident of both Contracting States, then it shall be deemed to be a resident of the State in which its place of effective management is situated.

Article 6 Income from immovable property

(1) Income derived by a resident of a Contracting State from immovable property (including income from agriculture or forestry) situated in the other Contracting State may be taxed in that other State.

Article 10 Dividends

(1) Dividends paid by a company which is a resident of a Contracting State to a resident of the other Contracting State may be taxed in that other State.

(2) However, such dividends may also be taxed in the Contracting State of which the company paying the dividends is a resident and according to the laws of that State, but if the recipient is the beneficial owner of the dividends the tax shall not exceed:

(a) 5% of the gross amount of the dividends if the beneficial owner is a company (other than a partnership) which holds directly at least 25% of the capital of the company paying the dividends;

(b) 15% of the gross amount of the dividends in all other cases.

The competent authorities of the Contracting States shall by mutual agreement settle the mode of application of these limitations.

This paragraph shall not affect the taxation of the company in respect of the profits out of which the dividends are paid.

Article 11 Interest

(1) Interest arising in a Contracting State and paid to a resident of the other Contracting State may be taxed in that other State.

(2) However, such interest may also be taxed in the Contracting State in which it arises and according to the laws of that State; but if the recipient is the beneficial owner of the interest the tax so charged shall not exceed 10% of the gross amount of the interest. The competent authorities of the Contracting State shall by mutual agreement settle the mode of application of this limitation.

Article 13 Capital gains

(1) Gains derived by a resident of a Contracting State from the alienation of immovable property referred to in Article 6 and situated in the other Contracting State may be taxed in that other State.

Article 14   Independent personal services

(1)   Income derived by a resident of a Contracting State in respect of professional services (or other activities of an independent character) shall be taxable only in that State unless he has a fixed base regularly available to him in the other Contracting State for the purpose of performing his activities. If he has such a fixed base, the income may be taxed in the other State but only so much of it as is attributable to that fixed base.

(2)   The term ''professional services'' includes especially independent scientific, literary, artistic, educational or teaching activities as well as the independent activities of physicians, lawyers, engineers, architects, dentists and accountants.

Article 15   Dependent personal services

(1)   Subject to the provisions of of Articles 16, 18 and 19, salaries, wages and other similar remuneration derived by a resident of a Contracting State in respect of an employment shall be taxable only in that State unless the employment is exercised in the other Contracting State. If the employment is so exercised, such remuneration as is derived therefrom may be taxed in that other state.

(2)   Notwithstanding the provisions of paragraph 1, remuneration derived by a resident of a Contracting State in respect of an employment exercised in the other Contracting State shall be taxable only in the first-mentioned State if:

    (a)   the recipient is present in the other State for a period or periods not exceeding in the aggregate 183 days in the fiscal year concerned, and

    (b)   the remuneration is paid by, or on behalf of, an employer who is not a resident of the other State, and

    (c)   the remuneration is not borne by a permanent establishment or a fixed base which the employer has in the other State.

(3)   Notwithstanding the preceding provisions of this Article, remuneration derived in respect of an employment exercised aboard a ship or aircraft operated in international traffic, or aboard a boat engaged in inland waterways transport, may be taxed in the Contracting State in which the place of effective management of the enterprise is situated.

Article 16   Directors' fees

Directors' fees and other similar payments derived by a resident of a Contracting State in his capacity as a member of the board of directors of a company which is a resident of the other Contracting State may be taxed in that other State.

Article 18   Pensions

Subject to the provisions of paragraph 2 of Article 19, pensions and other similar remuneration paid to a resident of a Contracting State in consideration of past employment shall be taxable only in that State.

Article 19 Government service

(1) (a) Remuneration, other than a pension, paid by a Contracting State or a political subdivision or a local authority thereof to an individual in respect of services rendered to that State or subdivision or authority shall be taxable only in that State.

    (b) However, such remuneration shall be taxable only in the other Contracting State if the services are rendered in that State and the individual is a resident of that State who:

        (i) is a national of that State; or

        (ii) did not become a resident of that State solely for the purpose of rendering the services.

(2) (a) Any pension paid by, or out of funds created by, a Contracting State or a political subdivision or a local authority thereof to an individual in respect of services rendered to that State or subdivision or authority shall be taxable in that State.

    (b) However, such pension shall be taxable only in the other Contracting State if the individual is a resident of, and a national of, that State.

(3) The provisions of Articles 15, 16 and 18 shall apply to remuneration and pensions in respect of services rendered in connection with a business carried on by a Contracting State or a political subdivision or a local authority thereof.

Article 26 Exchange of information

(1) *The competent authorities of the Contracting States shall exchange such information as is necessary for carrying out the provisions of this Convention or of the domestic laws of the Contracting States concerning taxes covered by the Convention insofar as the taxation thereunder is not contrary to the Convention. The exchange of information is not restricted by Article 1. Any information received by a Contracting State shall be treated as secret in the same manner as information obtained under the domestic laws of that State and shall be disclosed only to persons or authorities (including courts and administrative bodies) involved in the assessment or collection of, the enforcement or prosecution in respect of, or the determination of appeals in relation to, the taxes covered by the Convention.*

Directory of expatriate services

Firm/Company	Description of Services	Charges	Telephone/Telex

Portfolio Management Service

Firm/Company	Description of Services	Charges	Telephone/Telex
Capel-Cure Myers, (Members of the Stock Exchange) 65 Holborn Viaduct, London EC1A 2EV	A complete range of services, including investment management, tax advice, overseas settlements, investment holding companies etc.	On application	01-236 5080 Telex 886653 PROCUR Fax 01-329 4271 Contact: Alun Evans
Fidelity International (CI) Limited, 9 Bond Street, St Helier, Jersey, Channel Islands	Discretionary portfolio management service for international and UK-resident investors, using Fidelity's comprehensive range of offshore funds. Monthly transaction statements. Half yearly valuation and investment reports.	Standard initial charge on most deals. Sliding scale of initial charge for amounts of $100,000 or over. % annual fee. Switching charge usually 1% (reduced from 5%).	0534 71696 Telex 4192260 FICI G Fax 0534 31344 Contact: Howard de la Haye
Murray Noble (Financial Planners) Ltd Lonsdale Chambers, 27 Chancery Lane, London WC2A 1NF	Murray Noble is recognised as one of the leading firms of independent financial planners in the UK; offering a comprehensive range of services, from investment management and taxation to pension planning.	Preparation of personal reports (e.g. portfolio planning) from £75. Investment management 1.5% p.a.	01-405 6356 Contact: Phil Churchill
Skott & Stalker Ltd Overseas Investment Management, 59 Athol Street, Douglas, Isle of Man	Offshore investment counselling and portfolio management for clients large and small. Advice on establishment of offshore companies and trusts. Full nominee services available. Licensed by Isle of Man Government.	No charge for initial consultations. Minimum annual fee £150 includes regular revaluations and reviews.	0624 24440 Telex 629972 SANDS Contact: Peter Stalker
Warburg Investment Management Jersey Ltd, 39-41 Broad Street, St Helier, Jersey, Channel Islands	Discretionary portfolio management services for expatriates and international private clients, using either portfolios of in-house funds (minimum US$75,000 or sterling equivalent) or through direct equity investment (minimum US$500,000 or other currency equivalent).	1% p.a. subject to a minimum of US$750 p.a. for managed fund portfolios, US$5,000 for directly invested portfolios.	0534 74715 Telex 4192041 Contact: David Oldfield

ADVERTISERS' ANNOUNCEMENT

Firm/Company	Description of Services	Charges	Telephone/Telex
General Financial Services **Capel-Cure Myers,** (Members of the Stock Exchange) 65 Holborn Viaduct, London EC1A 2EV	A complete range of services, including investment management, tax advice, overseas settlements, investment holding companies etc.	On application	01-236 5080 Telex 886653 PROCUR Fax 01-329 4271 Contact: Alun Evans
Hill Samuel **Investment** **Services** **International SA,** Bureau de Representation, 10 rue Robert-Estienne, CH 1204 Geneva	Offshore funds – lump sum/ savings plan; offshore fund management service from £15,000; private client investment services from £200,000; tax planning, trusts and companies. Full Jersey/ Swiss banking facilities.	Offshore funds 5% initial charge. Offshore fund management service 0.2% p.a. (min £150, max £400) on value of portfolio. Private client investment service 0.5% p.a. (min £1,000) on value of portfolio.	010-41 22 21 25 55 Contact: Michael Vlahovic
MIM Britannia **International** **Limited,** PO Box 271, Queensway House, St Helier, Jersey, Channel Islands	International investment management of offshore funds and services for UK and international clients. The services available include discretionary portfolio management, share exchange and a high interest cheque account.	Minimum lump sum investment £1,000/ US$2,000 (except US Financial Institutions Fund: US$5,000). Minimum monthly savings: £50. Annual charges vary with each fund.	0534 73114 Telex 4192092 BRITTM G Fax 0534 73174 Contact: Deborah Sappé
NatWest Expatriate **Service,** National Westminster Bank Plc. Expatriate Service Office, PO Box 12 National Westminster House, 6 High Street, Chelmsford, Essex CM1 1BL	Provides the fullest support to expatriates in meeting their varied financial requirements whilst abroad. NatWest provides a full range of services including comprehensive banking facilities — in the UK and offshore; UK personal tax advice; savings accounts in sterling or currency; offshore funds or full investment management; mortgage and loan facilities and insurance advice. A packaged service for overseas corporates sending executives to the UK is available and, also for executives going to New York.	No charge is made by the expatriate service office acting as a co-ordinating office for the expatriate customer.	0245 261891 Fax 0245 490627
Skott & Stalker Ltd **Overseas** **Investment** **Management,** 59 Athol Street, Douglas, Isle of Man	Offshore investment counselling and portfolio management for clients large and small. Advice on establishment of offshore companies and trusts. Full nominee services available. Licensed by Isle of Man Government.	No charge for initial consultations. Minimum annual fee £150 includes regular revaluations and reviews.	0624 24440 Telex 629972 SANDS Contact: Peter Stalker

Firm/Company	Description of Services	Charges	Telephone/Telex

Banking Services

Tyndall Bank Limited, PO Box 62, Tyndall House, Kensington Road, Douglas, Isle of Man	Sterling and US Dollar Money Accounts — high interest deposit accounts with a cheque book. Gross interest and confidentiality of offshore bank. Fixed and currency deposits, nominee and investment services.		0624 28201 Telex 628732 Fax 0624 20200 Contact: Mr B J Tippett
A.L. Galliano Bankers Ltd, 76 Main Street, Gibraltar	Private bankers ideally placed to serve the needs of offshore clients. We deal with a worldwide network of correspondent banks. Personal and confidental services guaranteed.		72782 Telex 2215 & 2309 Fax 72732 Contact: Joseph M Olivero
The Royal Bank of Scotland (I.O.M.) Ltd, Victory House, Prospect Hill, Douglas, Isle of Man	High interest cheque account.	The first 10 withdrawals per quarter are free. Thereafter each withdrawal costs 35p.	0624 29111 Telex 628214 RBSIOM Fax 0624 72685 Contact: Andrew White
The Royal Bank of Scotland (I.O.M.) Ltd, Victory House, Prospect Hill, Douglas, Isle of Man	Sterling and currency deposit accounts at rates of interest based on the London and international money markets. Interest on deposits is paid gross without deduction of any income tax.		0624 29111 Telex 628214 RBSIOM Fax 0624 72685 Contact: Andrew White

Insurance/Investment Services

BUPA International, BUPA International Branch, 102 Queen's Road, Brighton BN1 3XT	BUPA International Lifetime is specially designed to provide British, and also Third Country National, expatriates under 65 with comprehensive cover against the heavy costs of medical treatment abroad, wherever they go.	Quotations available on request. Subscriptions payable either annually or quarterly.	0273 23563 Telex 877868 Fax 0273 820517 Contact: Mike Jones
ExpaCare Insurance Services, PO Box 71, Thames House, 1-4 Queen Street Place, London EC4R 1JA	Expatriate Medical Expenses Plan offering unlimited cover for hospital costs and outpatient treatment. ExpaCare is a wholly owned subsidiary of Jardine Insurance Brokers Ltd. Other insurance products are available.		01-489 1994 Telex 924093 Fax 01-236 3316 Contact: Debbie Purser

141

Index

Advertisers' Index